theolog MY

Siku

Batman is Jesus

PRINCESS
LOVER

WHORE
LOVER

Fortress Press
Minneapolis

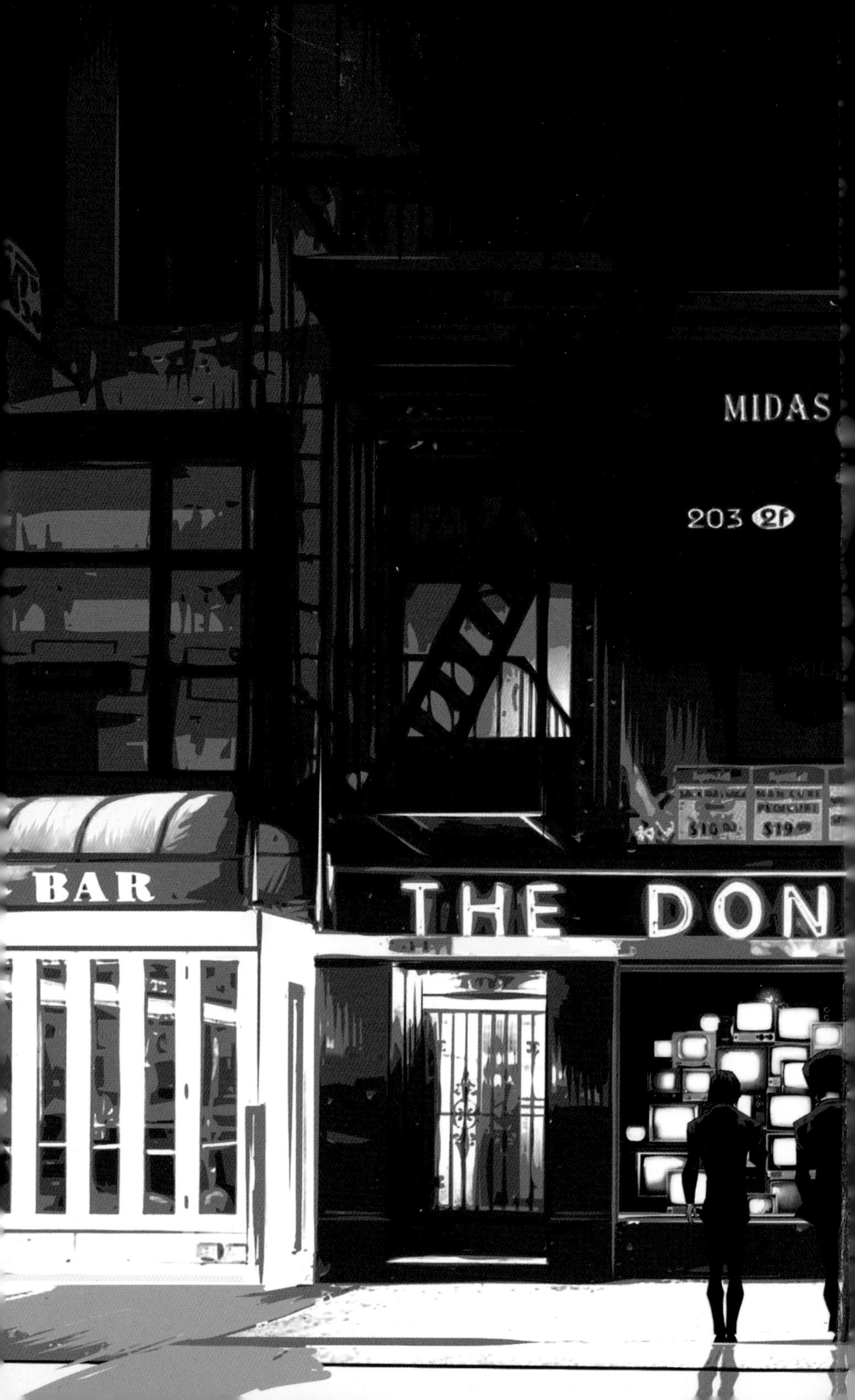
MIDAS
203
BAR
THE DON

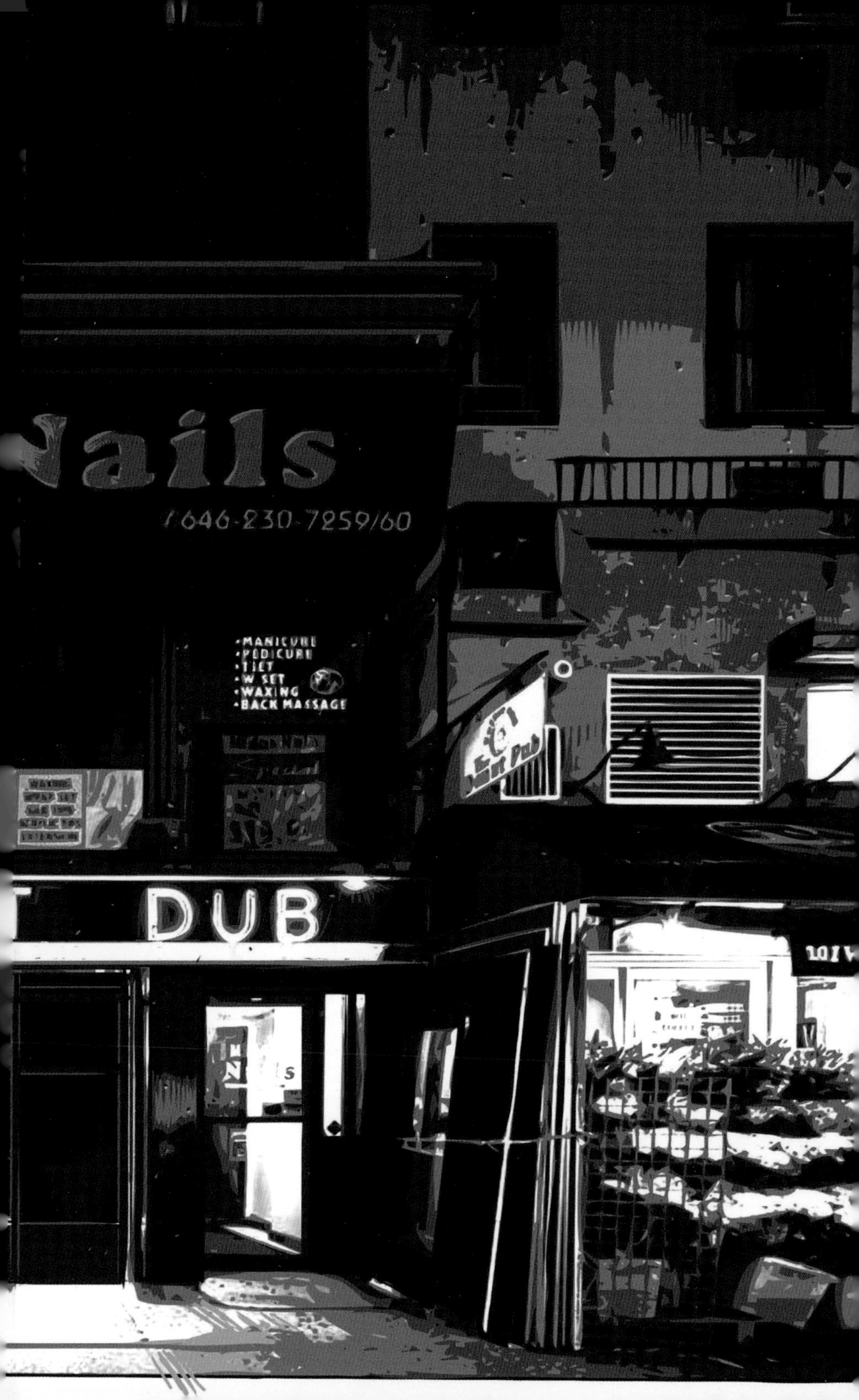

ails
646-230-7259/60
•MANICURE
•PEDICURE
•WAXING
•BACK MASSAGE
DUB

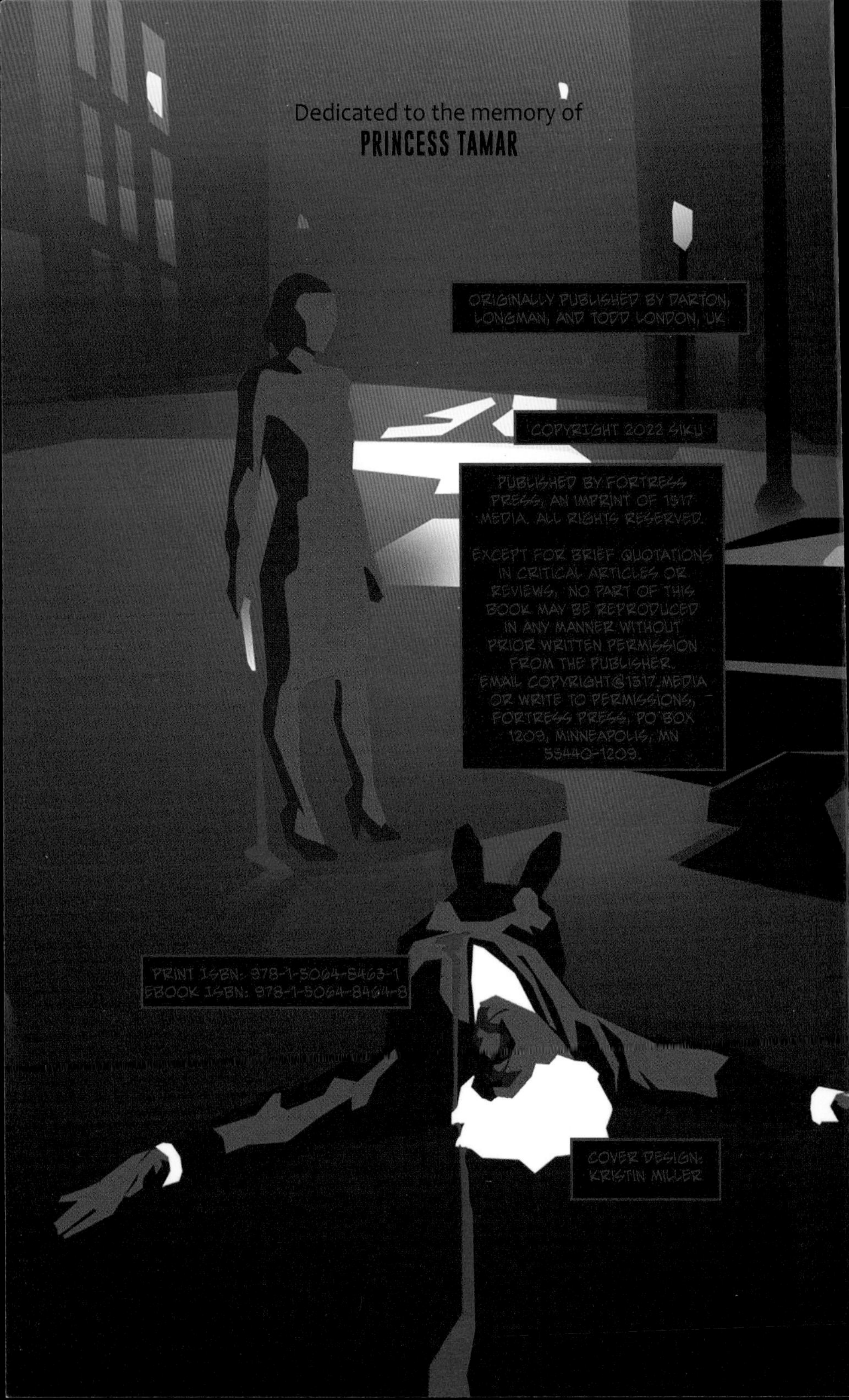

Dedicated to the memory of
PRINCESS TAMAR

ORIGINALLY PUBLISHED BY DARTON, LONGMAN, AND TODD LONDON, UK

PUBLISHED BY FORTRESS PRESS, AN IMPRINT OF 1517 MEDIA.

PRINT ISBN: 978-1-5064-8463-1
EBOOK ISBN: 978-1-5064-8464-8

COVER DESIGN: KRISTIN MILLER

CONTENTS

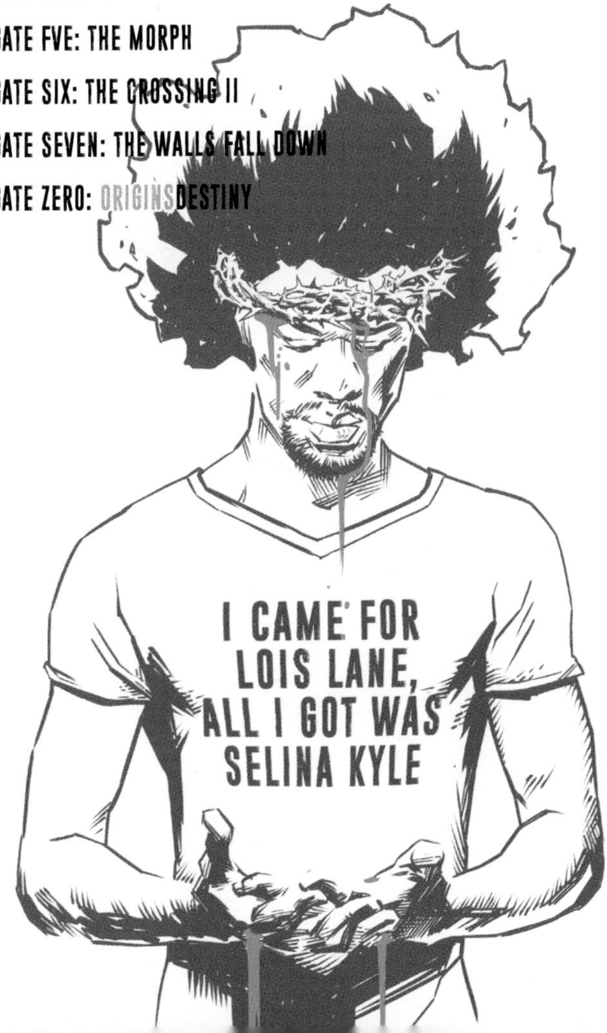

I CAME FOR LOIS LANE, ALL I GOT WAS SELINA KYLE

ORIGIN

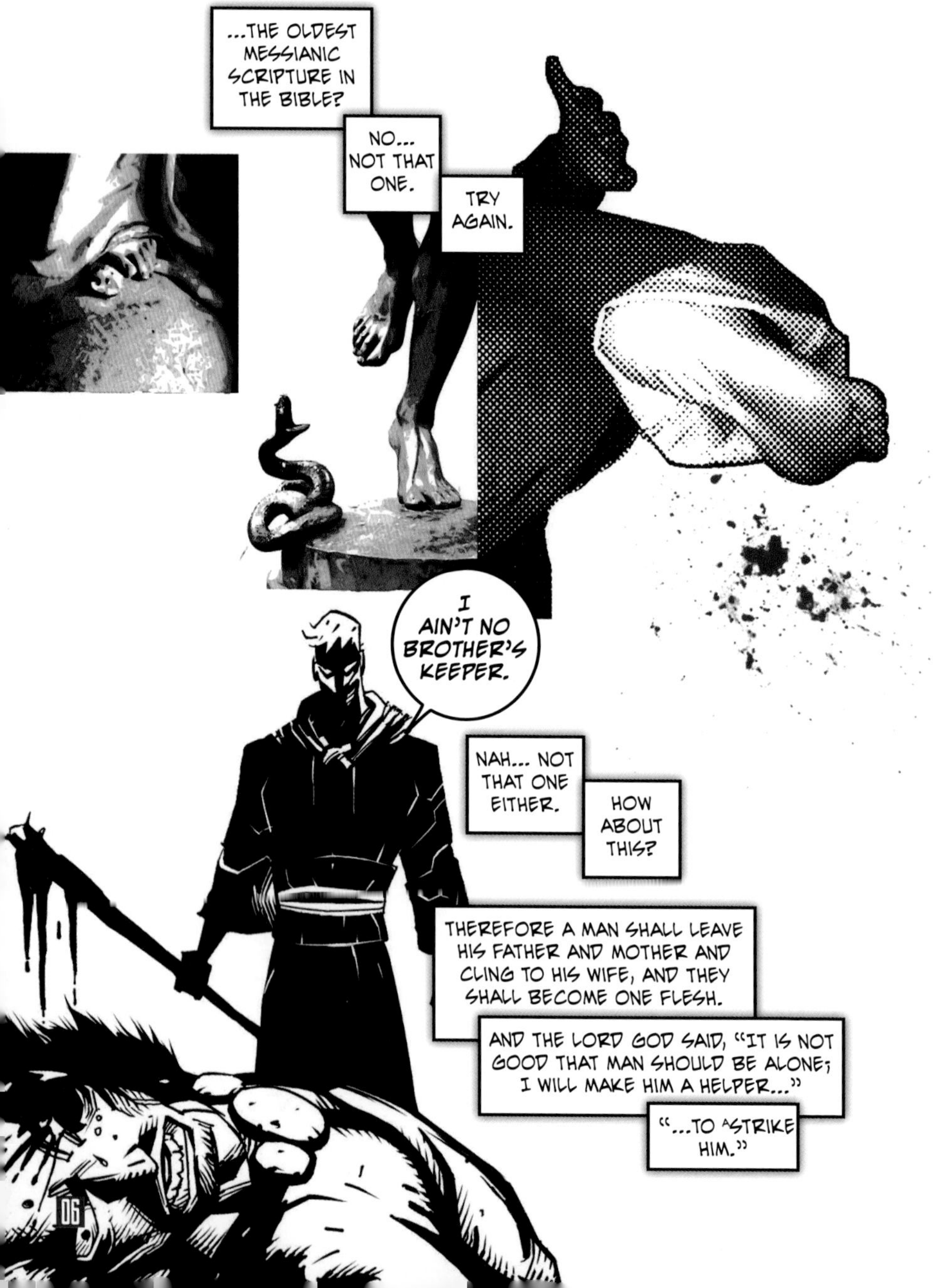
...THE OLDEST MESSIANIC SCRIPTURE IN THE BIBLE?
NO... NOT THAT ONE.
TRY AGAIN.
I AIN'T NO BROTHER'S KEEPER.
NAH... NOT THAT ONE EITHER.
HOW ABOUT THIS?
THEREFORE A MAN SHALL LEAVE HIS FATHER AND MOTHER AND CLING TO HIS WIFE, AND THEY SHALL BECOME ONE FLESH.
AND THE LORD GOD SAID, "IT IS NOT GOOD THAT MAN SHOULD BE ALONE; I WILL MAKE HIM A HELPER..."
"...TO STRIKE HIM."

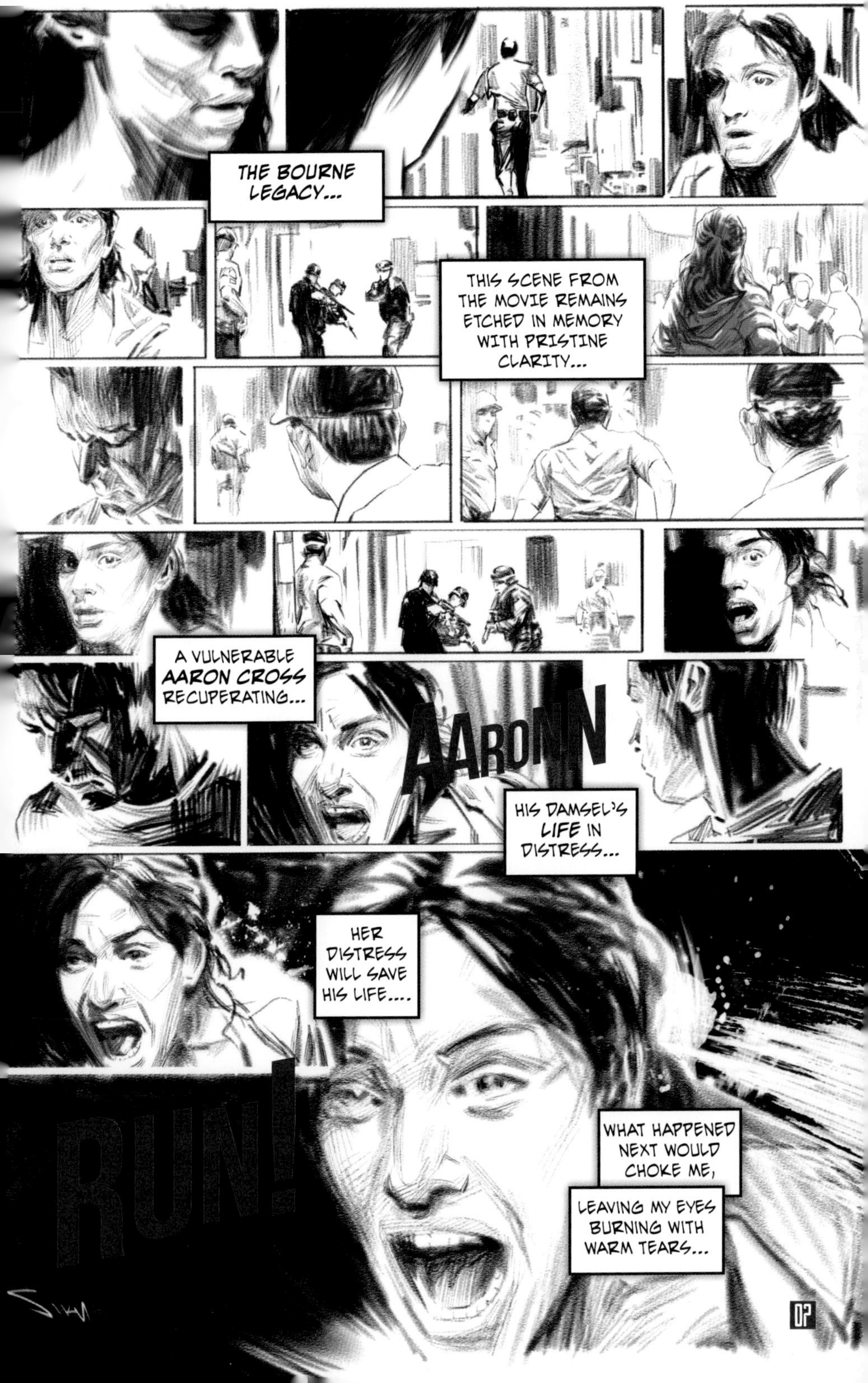

THE BOURNE LEGACY...
THIS SCENE FROM THE MOVIE REMAINS ETCHED IN MEMORY WITH PRISTINE CLARITY...
A VULNERABLE **AARON CROSS** RECUPERATING...
AARONN
HIS DAMSEL'S *LIFE* IN DISTRESS...
HER DISTRESS WILL SAVE HIS LIFE....
RUN!
WHAT HAPPENED NEXT WOULD CHOKE ME,
LEAVING MY EYES BURNING WITH WARM TEARS...

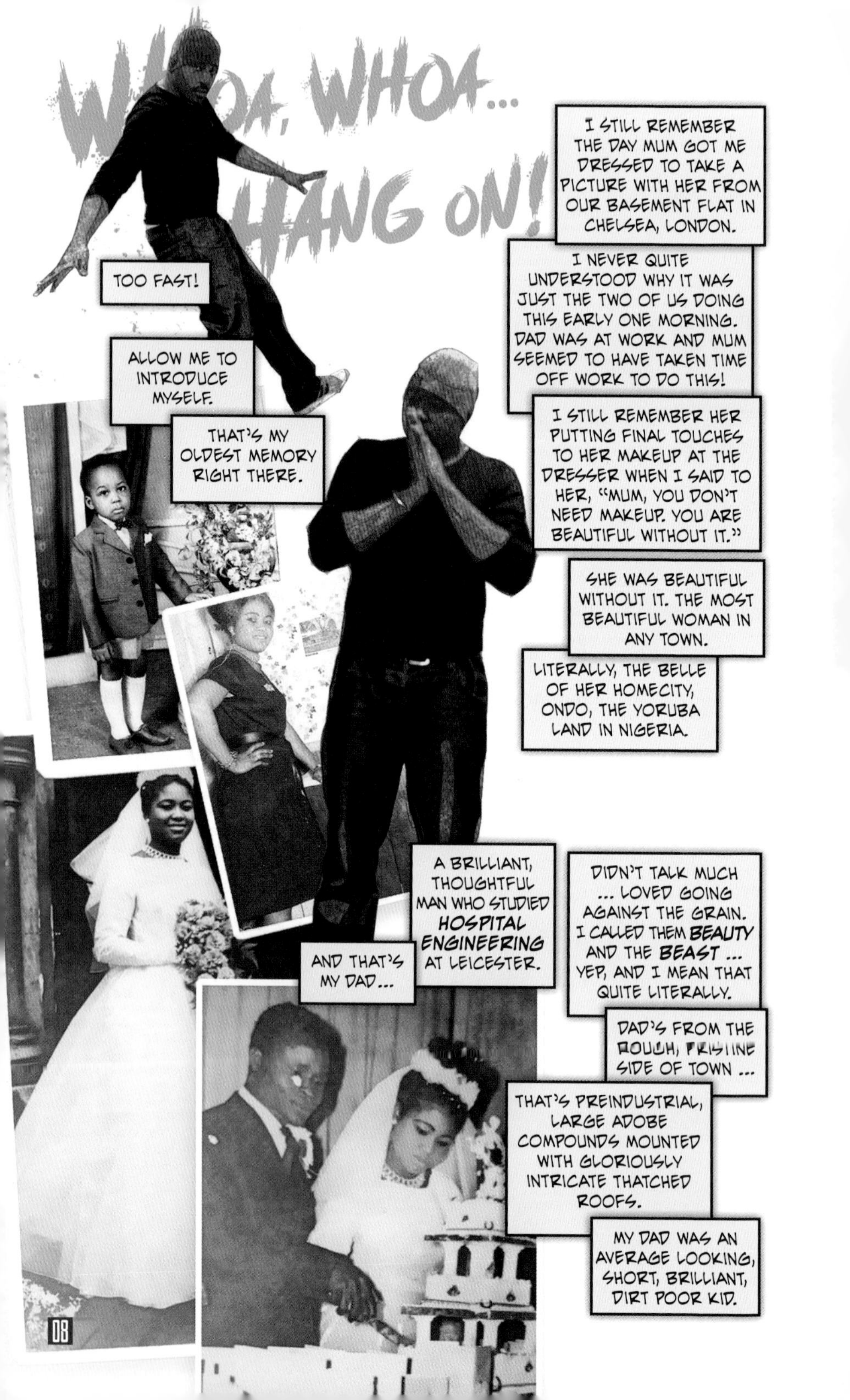
WHOA, WHOA... HANG ON!
TOO FAST!
ALLOW ME TO INTRODUCE MYSELF.
THAT'S MY OLDEST MEMORY RIGHT THERE.
I STILL REMEMBER THE DAY MUM GOT ME DRESSED TO TAKE A PICTURE WITH HER FROM OUR BASEMENT FLAT IN CHELSEA, LONDON.
I NEVER QUITE UNDERSTOOD WHY IT WAS JUST THE TWO OF US DOING THIS EARLY ONE MORNING. DAD WAS AT WORK AND MUM SEEMED TO HAVE TAKEN TIME OFF WORK TO DO THIS!
I STILL REMEMBER HER PUTTING FINAL TOUCHES TO HER MAKEUP AT THE DRESSER WHEN I SAID TO HER, "MUM, YOU DON'T NEED MAKEUP. YOU ARE BEAUTIFUL WITHOUT IT."
SHE WAS BEAUTIFUL WITHOUT IT. THE MOST BEAUTIFUL WOMAN IN ANY TOWN.
LITERALLY, THE BELLE OF HER HOMECITY, ONDO, THE YORUBA LAND IN NIGERIA.
AND THAT'S MY DAD...
A BRILLIANT, THOUGHTFUL MAN WHO STUDIED **HOSPITAL ENGINEERING** AT LEICESTER.
DIDN'T TALK MUCH ... LOVED GOING AGAINST THE GRAIN. I CALLED THEM **BEAUTY** AND THE **BEAST** ... YEP, AND I MEAN THAT QUITE LITERALLY.
DAD'S FROM THE ROUGH, PRISTINE SIDE OF TOWN ...
THAT'S PREINDUSTRIAL, LARGE ADOBE COMPOUNDS MOUNTED WITH GLORIOUSLY INTRICATE THATCHED ROOFS.
MY DAD WAS AN AVERAGE LOOKING, SHORT, BRILLIANT, DIRT POOR KID.
08

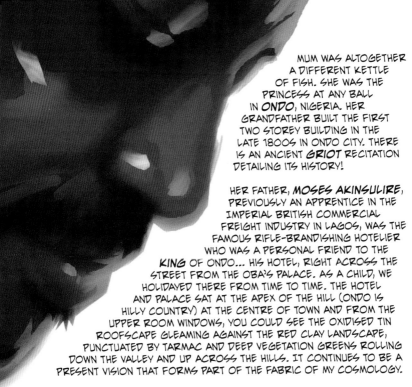

MUM WAS ALTOGETHER A DIFFERENT KETTLE OF FISH. SHE WAS THE PRINCESS AT ANY BALL IN **ONDO**, NIGERIA. HER GRANDFATHER BUILT THE FIRST TWO STOREY BUILDING IN THE LATE 1800S IN ONDO CITY. THERE IS AN ANCIENT **GRIOT** RECITATION DETAILING ITS HISTORY!

HER FATHER, **MOSES AKINSULIRE**, PREVIOUSLY AN APPRENTICE IN THE IMPERIAL BRITISH COMMERCIAL FREIGHT INDUSTRY IN LAGOS, WAS THE FAMOUS RIFLE-BRANDISHING HOTELIER WHO WAS A PERSONAL FRIEND TO THE **KING** OF ONDO... HIS HOTEL, RIGHT ACROSS THE STREET FROM THE OBA'S PALACE. AS A CHILD, WE HOLIDAYED THERE FROM TIME TO TIME. THE HOTEL AND PALACE SAT AT THE APEX OF THE HILL (ONDO IS HILLY COUNTRY) AT THE CENTRE OF TOWN AND FROM THE UPPER ROOM WINDOWS, YOU COULD SEE THE OXIDISED TIN ROOFSCAPE GLEAMING AGAINST THE RED CLAY LANDSCAPE, PUNCTUATED BY TARMAC AND DEEP VEGETATION GREENS ROLLING DOWN THE VALLEY AND UP ACROSS THE HILLS. IT CONTINUES TO BE A PRESENT VISION THAT FORMS PART OF THE FABRIC OF MY COSMOLOGY.

TO CLAIM THAT MY MUM HAD THE PICK OF THE MOST ELIGIBLE SUITORS WOULD REQUIRE NO LEAP OF IMAGINATION: FROM TIME TO TIME SHE WOULD BOAST,

"I DIDN'T CHOOSE YOUR DADDY FOR HIS LOOKS OR HIS MONEY ... I CHOSE HIM FOR HIS BRAINS! HE IS A BRILLIANT MAN."

DAD ON THE OTHER HAND ... **NO COMMENT.** I RARELY HEARD HIM VOICE HIS OPINION ON ANYTHING. WELL, EXCEPT FOR THE ODD MILITARY COUP REPLACING ANY GIVEN **CORRUPT** INCUMBENT CIVILIAN, DEMOCRATICALLY-ACCOUNTABLE AUTHORITY. WHILST OTHER NIGERIANS CELEBRATED THE TURNING OUT OF CORRUPT LEADERSHIP, MY FATHER WOULD QUIP, "SOLDIERS DON'T KNOW HOW TO GOVERN ... ALL THEY KNOW IS HOW TO SHOOT GUN".

ALONG WITH THE BROKEN ENGLISH, DESIGNED TO MOCK THE POORLY EDUCATED RANK AND FILE ARMY RECRUIT, THERE WAS A CYNICAL RESIGNATION IN HIS VOICE ... A RESIGNATION THAT ACCEPTED THE END OF A DREAM OF A YOUNG ENGINEER WHO TRAVELLED BACK TO HIS HOME COUNTRY TO HELP BUILD IT INTO A DEVELOPED NATION. **NIGERIA** HAD BECOME SYSTEMICALLY **CORRUPT**: SPIRITUALLY, CULTURALLY AND ECONOMICALLY BANKRUPT - AND MY FATHER LOOKED ON WITH AN IRONIC SHAKE OF THE HEAD.

THERE WAS SOMETHING ELSE THAT IRKED HIM; AND THIS, WE ARGUED ABOUT: HIS UTTER DISDAIN FOR WESTERN CHRISTIANITY. HIS EXPERIENCE WITH RACISM IN THE ANGLICAN CHURCH IN ENGLAND DECONSTRUCTED HIS ENTIRE CATECHISTIC UPBRINGING AS AN ANGLICAN. WE WERE AT ODDS TO BREAKING POINT ON THIS ISSUE; TO THE POINT OF CODED THREATS MADE TO A THIRTEEN YEAR OLD ... "DITCH CHRIST OR OUT".

THERE WAS ANOTHER MEMORY AS OLD AS ANY I CAN REMEMBER. WALKING INTO THE LIVING ROOM OF OUR BASEMENT FLAT WITH THE TV IN FRONT OF THE STREET FACING WINDOW, POWERED ON. ***DOCTOR WHO***, AS I CAME TO UNDERSTAND IT, WAS ON; MY FIRST CONSCIOUS ENCOUNTER WITH LIVE ACTION SCIENCE FICTION! THE DALEKS SCARED THE LIVING DAYLIGHTS OUT OF ME... HAUNTING, SCARY, DAZZLING ... I WAS MESMERISED ... GLUED TO EVERY DESIGN AND NARRATIVE ELEMENT DANCING OFF THE SCREEN. IT WAS THE LAST SEASON TO BE SHOT IN BLACK AND WHITE FEATURING THE SECOND DOCTOR, PATRICK TROUGHTON, ALTHOUGH TOM BAKER, THE FOURTH DOCTOR, WOULD BECOME THE DOCTOR OF MY GENERATION.

I STOOD HERE ... STRUCK IN AWE; THE CONNOTATIVE CONSTRUCTS IN MY MIND REMAIN WITH ME TILL THIS DAY AND IT GOES AS FOLLOWS ... IN GROWN UP WORDS,

"WHATEVER THAT IS, WHOEVER DID THAT, HOWEVER THAT WAS DONE ... THAT'S WHAT I WANT TO DO WHEN I GROW UP!"

THE TELEVISION SCREENS ON THE COVER OF THIS BOOK ARE SYMBOLIC OF THE SINGLE MOST IMPRESSIVE TECHNOLOGY IN THE FRAMEWORK OF THE PERSONALITY OF THIS AUTHOR. EVENTUALLY, I WOULD MOVE ON TO OTHER HIGHER BUDGET PRODUCTIONS LIKE ***STAR TREK, LOST IN SPACE, THE TWILIGHT ZONE, THE WILD WILD WEST***, ... AND THEN ***STAR WARS*** WHICH BROKE THE MOULD IN MORE WAYS.

I QUICKLY DISCOVERED COMICS JUST AFTER DISCOVERING SCIENCE FICTION TOYS; THE NARRATIVE WAS NOW IN MY CONTROL! I COULD READ IT AT MY PACE, THE STORIES NOW INHABITED AN EXPANSIVE DOMAIN IN MY MIND. MY DAD WOULD PICK ME UP FROM SCHOOL EVERYDAY ... ON OUR WAY HOME, JUST AS WE CROSSED THE LAST JUNCTION BEFORE HITTING HOME, STOOD THE LOCAL NEWSAGENCY ... MY IDEA OF HEAVEN AT THE TIME.

"DADDY, DADDY, BUY ME COMIC BOOK," I DEMANDED. THE WORD "PLEASE" HAD NOT YET FEATURED AS A STRATEGIC DEVICE IN MY TOOL BOX LABELLED, "HOW TO GET PEOPLE TO DO THINGS FOR YOU".

DAD DUTIFULLY OBLIGED. HE BOUGHT ME A COMIC BOOK EVERY SCHOOL DAY! ***BUNTY, BUSTER AND COR, DANDY, SUPERMAN ... BATMAN.*** I COULDN'T GET ENOUGH OF THE STUFF. WE GET TO MOVE ON FROM CHILDISH THINGS, DON'T WE? WE GRADUATED TO CHEAP HONG KONG MARTIAL MOVIES AND INDIAN MOVIES; MARTIAL ARTS WOULD BECOME ANOTHER PREOCCUPATION OF MINE, EVENTUALLY ENROLLING IN A KUNG FU AND KARATE CLUB. I DID SAY WE LEAVE CHILDISH THINGS DIDN'T I? THAT HAPPENS UNLESS YOU ARE A GEEK ... LIKE ME.

SOME BEGIN TO NOTICE GIRLS... YEAH, I KIND OF GOT IT... BUT AS A SLOW DEVELOPER I DISCOVERED READING INSTEAD; EVERYTHING FROM ISAAC ASIMOV TO LOBSANG RAMPA, BIOGRAPHIES OF GREAT MEN. AND THEN, AT AGE 18, I REDISCOVERED CHRIST, HAVING FIRST MET HIM AT THE AGE OF 11.

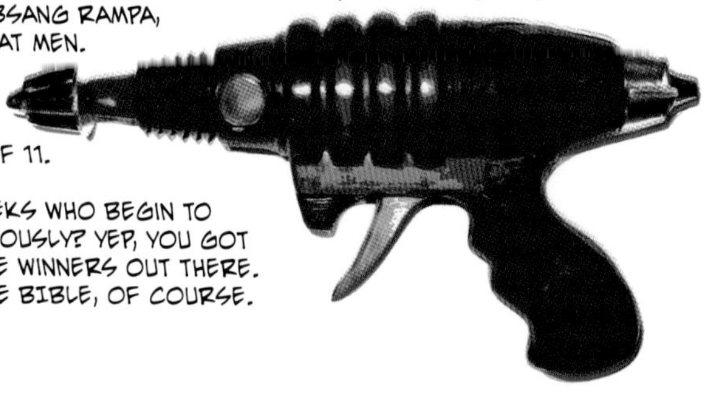

WHAT HAPPENS TO GEEKS WHO BEGIN TO TAKE THEIR FAITH SERIOUSLY? YEP, YOU GOT IT; NO PRIZES FOR THE WINNERS OUT THERE. THEY GEEK OUT ON THE BIBLE, OF COURSE.

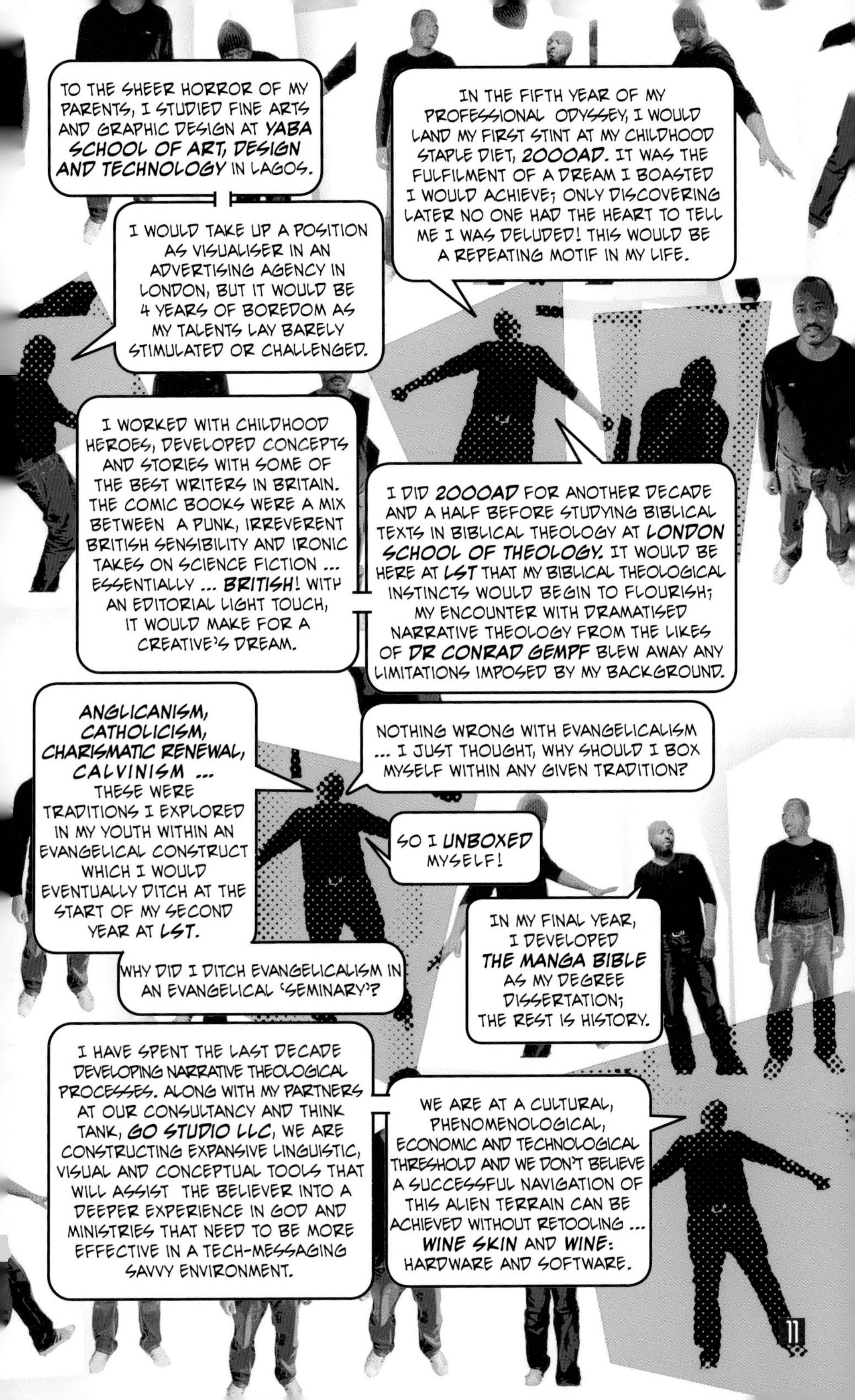
TO THE SHEER HORROR OF MY PARENTS, I STUDIED FINE ARTS AND GRAPHIC DESIGN AT YABA SCHOOL OF ART, DESIGN AND TECHNOLOGY IN LAGOS.
I WOULD TAKE UP A POSITION AS VISUALISER IN AN ADVERTISING AGENCY IN LONDON, BUT IT WOULD BE 4 YEARS OF BOREDOM AS MY TALENTS LAY BARELY STIMULATED OR CHALLENGED.
IN THE FIFTH YEAR OF MY PROFESSIONAL ODYSSEY, I WOULD LAND MY FIRST STINT AT MY CHILDHOOD STAPLE DIET, 2000AD. IT WAS THE FULFILMENT OF A DREAM I BOASTED I WOULD ACHIEVE; ONLY DISCOVERING LATER NO ONE HAD THE HEART TO TELL ME I WAS DELUDED! THIS WOULD BE A REPEATING MOTIF IN MY LIFE.
I WORKED WITH CHILDHOOD HEROES, DEVELOPED CONCEPTS AND STORIES WITH SOME OF THE BEST WRITERS IN BRITAIN. THE COMIC BOOKS WERE A MIX BETWEEN A PUNK, IRREVERENT BRITISH SENSIBILITY AND IRONIC TAKES ON SCIENCE FICTION ... ESSENTIALLY ... BRITISH! WITH AN EDITORIAL LIGHT TOUCH, IT WOULD MAKE FOR A CREATIVE'S DREAM.
I DID 2000AD FOR ANOTHER DECADE AND A HALF BEFORE STUDYING BIBLICAL TEXTS IN BIBLICAL THEOLOGY AT LONDON SCHOOL OF THEOLOGY. IT WOULD BE HERE AT LST THAT MY BIBLICAL THEOLOGICAL INSTINCTS WOULD BEGIN TO FLOURISH; MY ENCOUNTER WITH DRAMATISED NARRATIVE THEOLOGY FROM THE LIKES OF DR CONRAD GEMPF BLEW AWAY ANY LIMITATIONS IMPOSED BY MY BACKGROUND.
ANGLICANISM, CATHOLICISM, CHARISMATIC RENEWAL, CALVINISM ... THESE WERE TRADITIONS I EXPLORED IN MY YOUTH WITHIN AN EVANGELICAL CONSTRUCT WHICH I WOULD EVENTUALLY DITCH AT THE START OF MY SECOND YEAR AT LST.
WHY DID I DITCH EVANGELICALISM IN AN EVANGELICAL 'SEMINARY'?
NOTHING WRONG WITH EVANGELICALISM ... I JUST THOUGHT, WHY SHOULD I BOX MYSELF WITHIN ANY GIVEN TRADITION?
SO I UNBOXED MYSELF!
IN MY FINAL YEAR, I DEVELOPED THE MANGA BIBLE AS MY DEGREE DISSERTATION; THE REST IS HISTORY.
I HAVE SPENT THE LAST DECADE DEVELOPING NARRATIVE THEOLOGICAL PROCESSES. ALONG WITH MY PARTNERS AT OUR CONSULTANCY AND THINK TANK, GO STUDIO LLC, WE ARE CONSTRUCTING EXPANSIVE LINGUISTIC, VISUAL AND CONCEPTUAL TOOLS THAT WILL ASSIST THE BELIEVER INTO A DEEPER EXPERIENCE IN GOD AND MINISTRIES THAT NEED TO BE MORE EFFECTIVE IN A TECH-MESSAGING SAVVY ENVIRONMENT.
WE ARE AT A CULTURAL, PHENOMENOLOGICAL, ECONOMIC AND TECHNOLOGICAL THRESHOLD AND WE DON'T BELIEVE A SUCCESSFUL NAVIGATION OF THIS ALIEN TERRAIN CAN BE ACHIEVED WITHOUT RETOOLING ... WINE SKIN AND WINE: HARDWARE AND SOFTWARE.

... SO I WENT TO SPEAK AT ETON COLLEGE, WHERE I SPOKE ABOUT BITCHES, THE BLUES AND THE MOST TRAGIC SUPERHERO, EVER ... THE BATMAN!

I have seen those expressions of bewilderment before. Everyone posed with this question has that same look:

"What is the greatest tragedy to befall a hero?"

It felt like a random question for any given set of answers; some of the boys trotted out the usual replies, "Fails to save the world?", "Defeated by the bad guy?" Some *smarty pants* ingeniously suggested, "Turned to the *dark side?*"

It was greeted with laughter and applause ... "Nice try", I quipped. Then I expanded the dilemma, "Heroes can recover from losing a battle. I am talking about an unrecoverable, pathological failure ... there is only one right answer to the question." It is the query of the existential gut – the query of queries, stretching out for fleeting answers from another world ... here and yet, not here.

I take them through the roll call of tragic heroes; James Bond, Bruce Banner, Jack Bauer, The Ghost Rider. Note what they all have in common and when you add Bruce Wayne to the top of that list, you might begin to understand the direction of travel here.

The story of tragedy is one story. The same story is told with minor alterations by a thousand storytellers over a thousand years.

Each transmission carries with it an imprint of its collective authors. Yet, in all its guises, it remains the same story and that story defines the very core of our humanity in ways that are beyond mere words. Words – so inadequate a facility when it comes to speaking about truth and meaning to the extent that they reduce meaning by default – the essence of your meaning starts to degrade as soon as you begin to utter words to express your meaning.

It is astonishing that we have *gotten by* rather successfully (relatively speaking, of course) by means of such inefficient carriers of meaning... At least, if you are a dedicated reductionist materialist, content with the constant barrage of cognitive dissonance that you must contend with in order to remain sane, *it is astonishing*! That is to say, those who boast in the confidence of words, of logic and measurement, must contend with the fact that they find true meaning, peace, joy and contentment in/through things that are beyond expression in words and measurement.

For those of us more comfortable with our inadequacy to access the depth of meaning, we are content to use stories to convey meaning... expansively. For when we tell you a story, it will carry an imprint from your consciousness (or unconsciousness) that will alter that story... and yet, the story will remain essentially true... because that is the nature of Story.

It is that nature of malleability that contextualises our inconsistencies, inadequacies, idiosyncrasies, anachronistic impulses and self-implosion; to contextualise and to provide a marketplace in which to probe these impulses with others in the search for meaning and actualisation.

Some stories will fall by the wayside, some will be successful. So successful that they become folklore, the less successful falling onto footpaths like discarded seeds to be trampled under foot by passing traffic. The very best will rise to the surface; each iteration continues with the very best and total iterations seen in the Holy Bible. Cain and Abel; Adam, Eve, the Serpent and the Garden; Giant killing David; the General Deborah, Baby Moses; Esther; Ruth; Daniel in the Lion's Den; A Nation Exiled; the Return of the King; Jesus and apocalyptic imagery … the list goes on. The embodiment of archetypes in narratives were so designed by the Word of God – himself, the first letter of the first word uttered in any story, either in contempt or in adoration – narratives, designed to accurately capture the essence of being and reality, for it is impossible to lie when you tell a story.

We rediscovered our heritage (the Latin Church) in narrative speech through the literary critical works of [B]Northrope Frye (1957), [C]Robert Alter (1933 & 1981), [D]David Rhoads (1982), [E]Walter Fisher (1987) and [F]Alan Culpepper (1983). It might be noteworthy to cite French post-structuralists like [G]Roland Barth who developed 'reader response' models. Much of the new cultural shifts we see in the West are due to the implementation of literary deconstruction and the Church is not quite geared up for response, not to speak of a no holds barred frontal engagement.

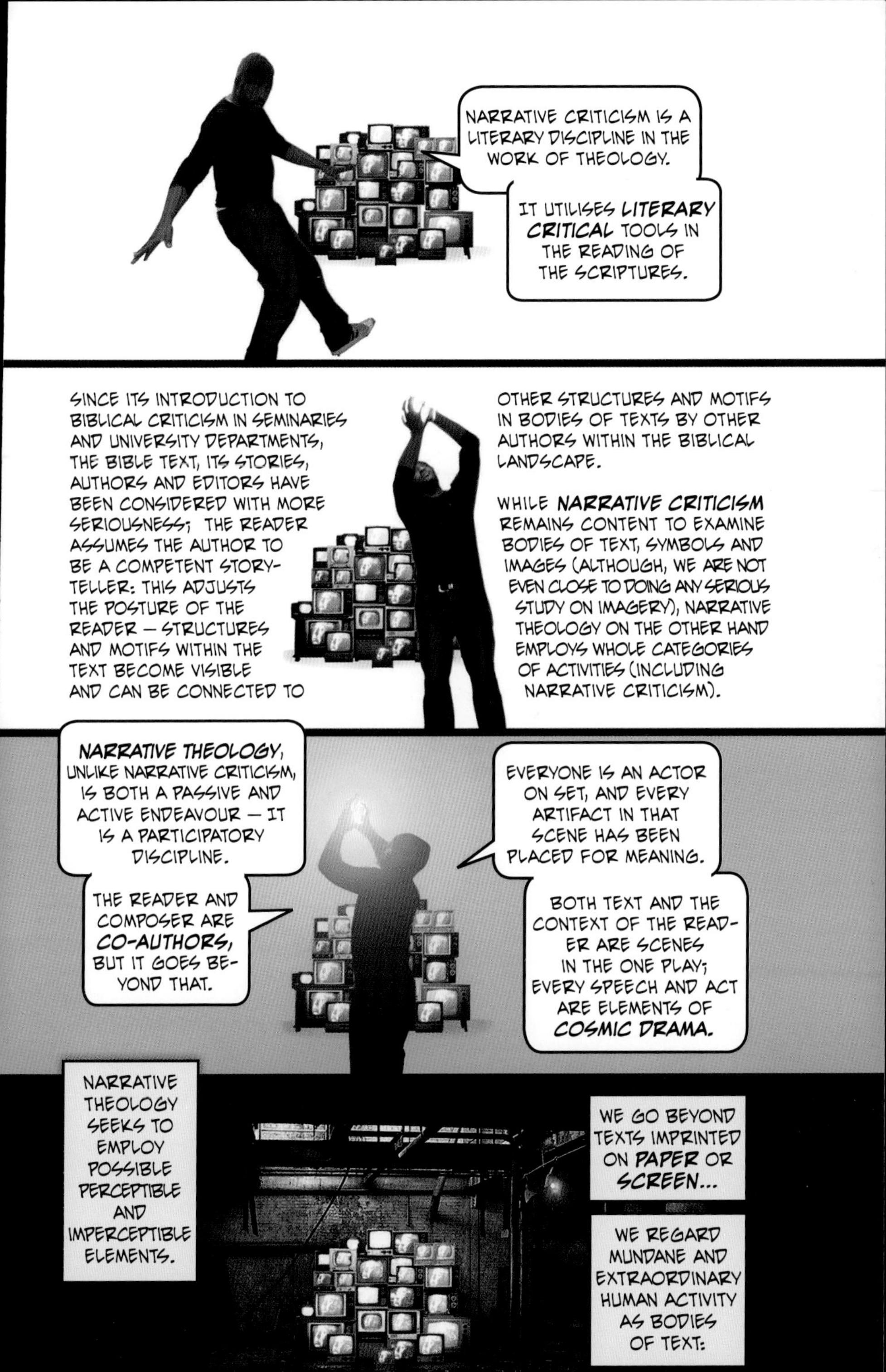
NARRATIVE CRITICISM IS A LITERARY DISCIPLINE IN THE WORK OF THEOLOGY.
IT UTILISES ***LITERARY CRITICAL*** TOOLS IN THE READING OF THE SCRIPTURES.
SINCE ITS INTRODUCTION TO BIBLICAL CRITICISM IN SEMINARIES AND UNIVERSITY DEPARTMENTS, THE BIBLE TEXT, ITS STORIES, AUTHORS AND EDITORS HAVE BEEN CONSIDERED WITH MORE SERIOUSNESS; THE READER ASSUMES THE AUTHOR TO BE A COMPETENT STORY-TELLER: THIS ADJUSTS THE POSTURE OF THE READER — STRUCTURES AND MOTIFS WITHIN THE TEXT BECOME VISIBLE AND CAN BE CONNECTED TO OTHER STRUCTURES AND MOTIFS IN BODIES OF TEXTS BY OTHER AUTHORS WITHIN THE BIBLICAL LANDSCAPE.
WHILE ***NARRATIVE CRITICISM*** REMAINS CONTENT TO EXAMINE BODIES OF TEXT, SYMBOLS AND IMAGES (ALTHOUGH, WE ARE NOT EVEN CLOSE TO DOING ANY SERIOUS STUDY ON IMAGERY), NARRATIVE THEOLOGY ON THE OTHER HAND EMPLOYS WHOLE CATEGORIES OF ACTIVITIES (INCLUDING NARRATIVE CRITICISM).
NARRATIVE THEOLOGY, UNLIKE NARRATIVE CRITICISM, IS BOTH A PASSIVE AND ACTIVE ENDEAVOUR — IT IS A PARTICIPATORY DISCIPLINE.
THE READER AND COMPOSER ARE ***CO-AUTHORS,*** BUT IT GOES BE-YOND THAT.
EVERYONE IS AN ACTOR ON SET, AND EVERY ARTIFACT IN THAT SCENE HAS BEEN PLACED FOR MEANING.
BOTH TEXT AND THE CONTEXT OF THE READ-ER ARE SCENES IN THE ONE PLAY; EVERY SPEECH AND ACT ARE ELEMENTS OF ***COSMIC DRAMA.***
NARRATIVE THEOLOGY SEEKS TO EMPLOY POSSIBLE PERCEPTIBLE AND IMPERCEPTIBLE ELEMENTS.
WE GO BEYOND TEXTS IMPRINTED ON ***PAPER*** OR ***SCREEN...***
WE REGARD MUNDANE AND EXTRAORDINARY HUMAN ACTIVITY AS BODIES OF TEXT:

		TO PROTECT A SECRET...	
THE WAVING OF THE ARM TO GREET A FRIEND...	THE BITING OF THE BOTTOM LIP,		THE ADOPTION OF THE FOETAL POSITION WHEN IN EMOTIONAL ANGUISH.

AT OUR CONSULTANCY AT GO STUDIO, WE ARE DEVELOPING A GRAPHIC THEOLOGY; VISUAL MAPS THAT PROVIDE SNAPSHOTS OF SPIRITUAL PHENOMENOLOGY. WE READ ALL MATERIALS AS BODIES OF TEXT, WHETHER CRAFTED BY THE HANDS OF HUMANS OR BY THE ARMS OF GOD. EVERYTHING IS PERFORMANCE ... EVERYTHING IS TEXT AND THIS FRAMING CAUSES THE NARRATIVE THEOLOGIAN TO ADOPT A PROPHETIC POSTURE.

THE DISCIPLINE OF NARRATIVE THEOLOGY BREAKS BEYOND THE BOUNDARIES OF BIBLICAL TEXT; LIKE SAINT PAUL, WE ASSUME THAT THE LAW IS ⁴IMPRINTED EVERYWHERE... RIGHT DOWN TO THE ELUSIVE PHENOMENON CALLED THE HUMAN HEART. SO WE READ THE WORLD AS THOUGH IT WERE BIBLICAL TEXT.

NOW, WHEN YOU READ THE MATERIAL AND IMMATERIAL WORLD AS THOUGH IT WERE PART OF THE MATRIX OF BIBLICAL REVELATION... WHAT DOES THAT DO TO THE SPEECH AND SPIRITUALITY OF THE PROPHET, THE CHRISTIAN CREATIVE, THE EVANGELIST?

IN THIS VOLUME, WE SEE SOME OF THAT THOUGHT IN ACTION: THE MAPPING OF JOURNEY AND HOW GOD'S PROVIDENCE CAUSES MEANING IN EVERYTHING.

THIS IS MY THEOLOGY.

REFERENCES

A.   Compare with Rashi's literal translation of Genesis 2:18 'make him a helper opposite him'. See *Yevamot 63a* for arguments of the rabbis.

B.   Frye, Northrop. 1957. *Anatomy of Criticism: Four Essays*, Princeton, Princeton University Press. A leading contribution to literary discussion before the advent of deconstructuralism and post-structuralism.

C.   Alter, Robert. 1981. *The Art of Biblical Narrative*, New York, Basic Books, See use of 'Type Scene'.

D.   Rhoads, David, and Donald Michie. 1982. *Mark as Story: An Introduction to the Narrative of a Gospel*. Minneapolis: Fortress Press. Rhoads invented the term, 'Narrative Criticism'.

E.   Walter Fisher introduced the narrative paradigm theory to communication theory. *Human Communication as Narration: Toward a Philosophy of Reason, Value and Action (Studies in Rhetoric and Communications)*, 1987.

F.   Culpepper , Alan. 1983. *Anatomy of the Fourth Gospel: A Study in Literary Design*, Philadelphia, Fortress Press. He introduced the role of the narrator POV in discussion of the Gospel of John.

G.   Barth, Roland. 1967. *The Death of The Author*. Most well known post-structuralists are Jacques Derrida, Michel Foucault, Gilles Deleuze, Judith Butler, Jean Baudrillard and Julia Kristeva. They are also known as 'diachronic' postmodernist thinkers; 'Diachronic' (historical, post-structure/post-binary/evolutionary)   vs 'Synchronic' (descriptive/stable) structuralist. See Foucalt's *Madness and Civilisation*.

H.   Romans 10:7-8, Deuteronomy 30:14, Romans 2:14,26-27, Romans 1:20-22.

GATE ZERO

ORIGINSDESTINY

KANSAS

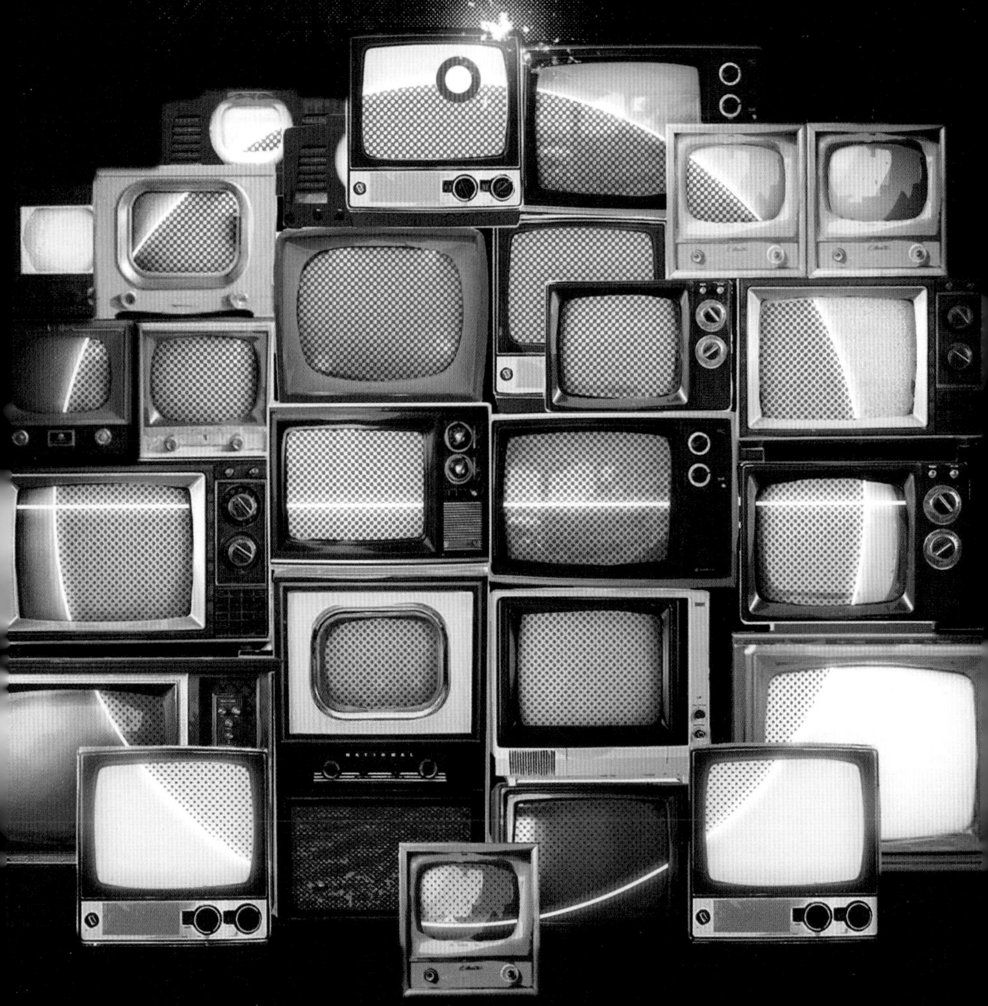

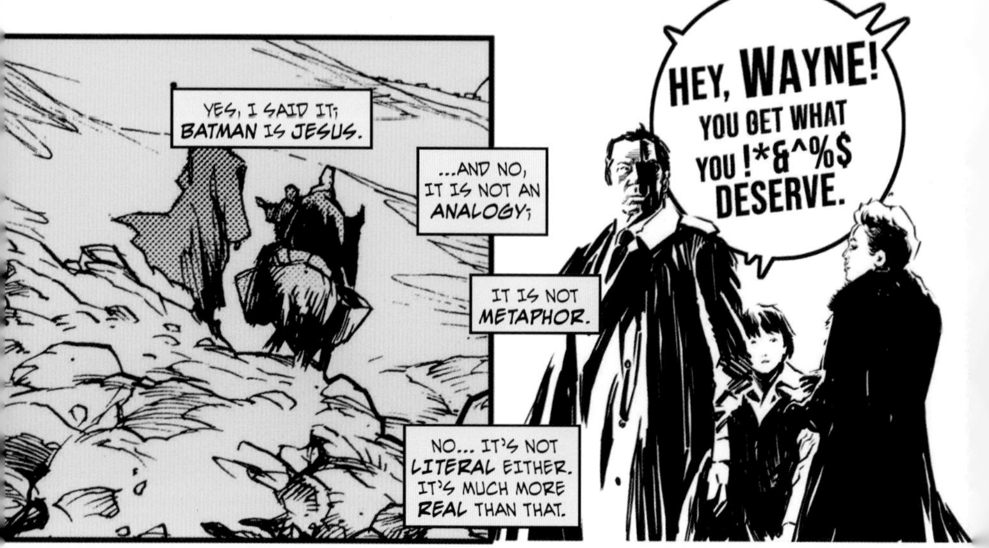
YES, I SAID IT; BATMAN IS JESUS.
...AND NO, IT IS NOT AN ANALOGY;
IT IS NOT METAPHOR.
NO... IT'S NOT LITERAL EITHER. IT'S MUCH MORE REAL THAN THAT.
HEY, WAYNE! YOU GET WHAT YOU !*&^%$ DESERVE.

Origins and Identity.

How is it that origins and identity must be forged in fire?

The conceiving, measuring, designing, banging, scraping, manipulating and tempering; every procedure requiring the allotted time, heat and pressure; nothing more, nothing less.

And then the deed is done ...

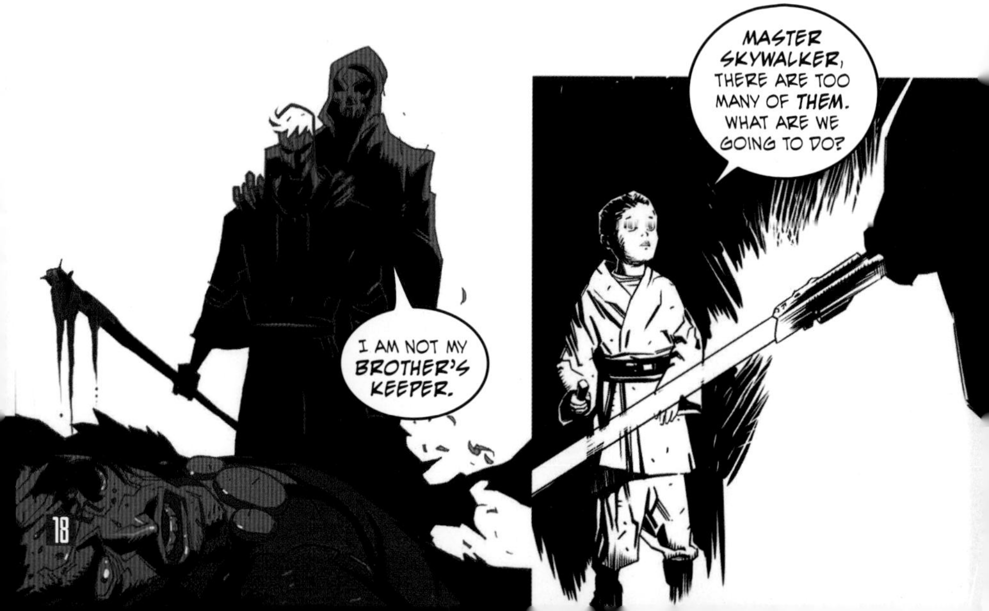
I AM NOT MY BROTHER'S KEEPER.
MASTER SKYWALKER, THERE ARE TOO MANY OF THEM. WHAT ARE WE GOING TO DO?

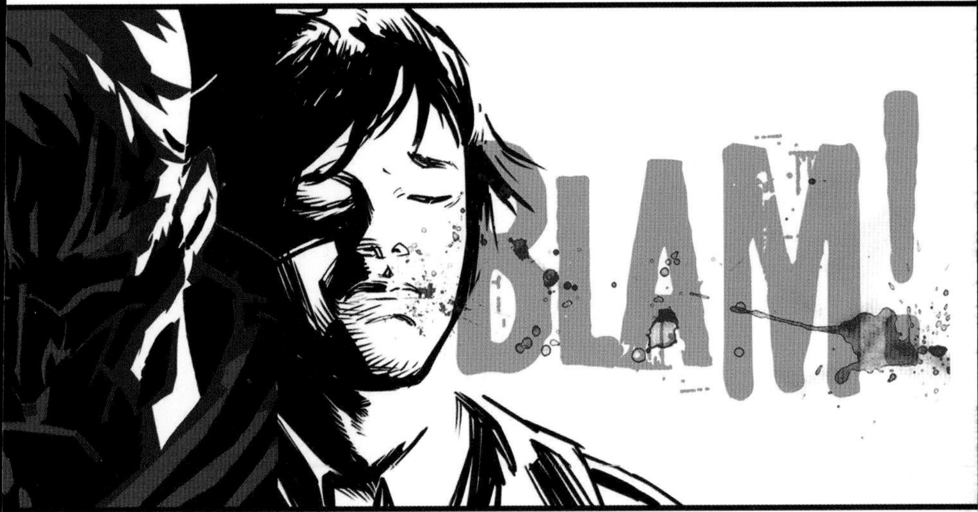
BLAM!

And this, still red hot, fabrication is indelibly registered with a mark. The mark of the forger and the mark of the forged.

[1]This mark is commonly known as, 'Identity'. You see, name and identity are virtually indistinguishable. This primitive act of mark-making itself; the first cited instance of writing in human history, is a mark of the villain, the hero, humanity itself, and eventually, the mark of the messiah himself.

An artificial mark, so primitive ... so simple, that it requires no description. It is a sublime, archetypal and defining inscription. This forging of writing itself is to be discovered in the foundry that is the human condition and human identity.

The metallurgist is not immune to the unforgiving foundry conditions; the burning heat, austere working conditions and risk of grave injury keeps the experienced alchemist alert.

Both forger and the forged will be altered by a dangerous intimacy; sometimes, the engineer and the engineered –the marker and the marked, will become virtually indistinguishable. The identity of one is menacingly mirrored in the identity of the other.

The villain and hero are forever stained by the indelible mark of premeditated murder. The murder of the innocents would forever extinguish old identities; Herod, Skywalker,

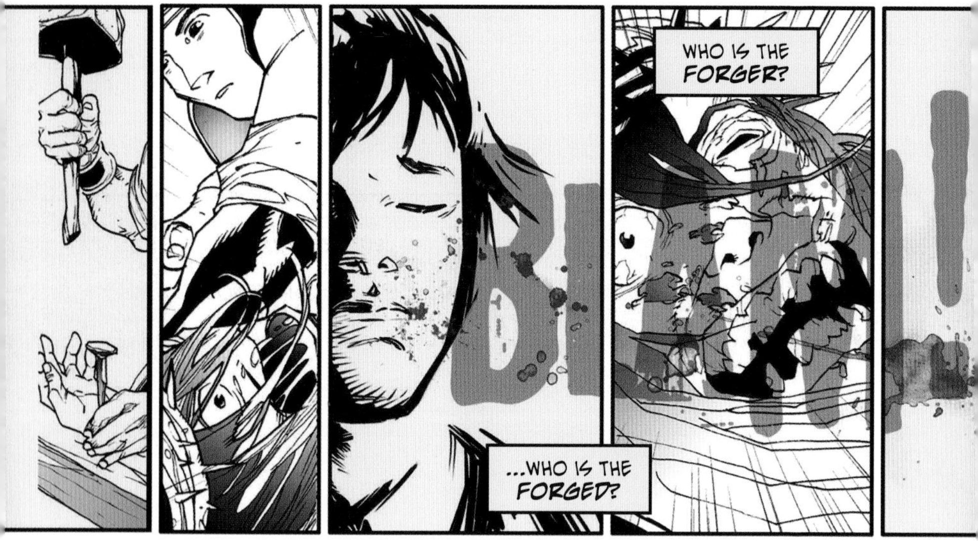
WHO IS THE FORGER?
...WHO IS THE FORGED?

Macbeth ... Cain. They would carry the primordial scar which marks both villain and hero: 'the bruised heel and the crushed head' – for the blood of one's slain parent splattered on the cheek, cannot be so easily dismissed.

You see, the messiah must become an intractable reverse reflection of the villain. He is... his brother's keeper.

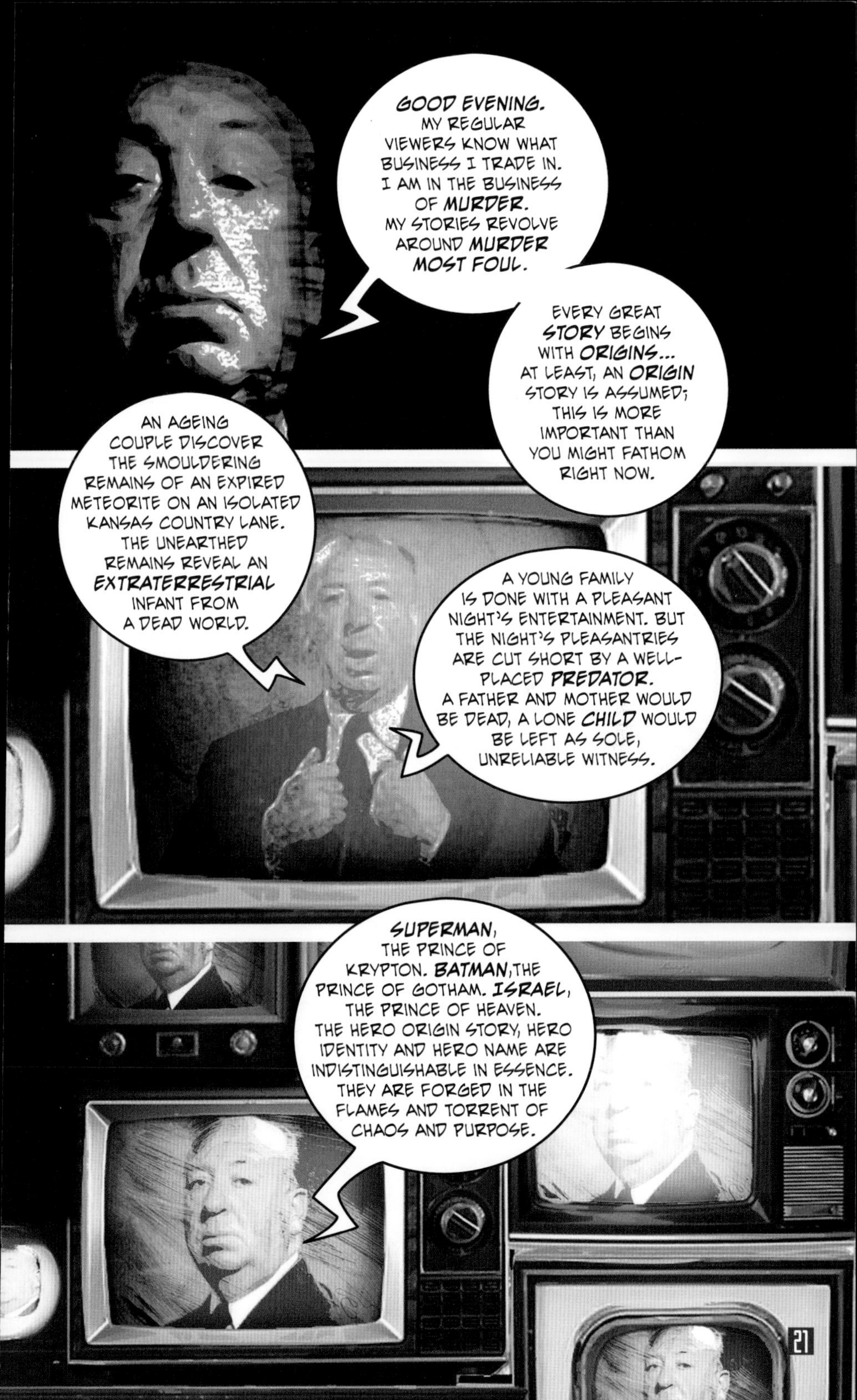
GOOD EVENING. MY REGULAR VIEWERS KNOW WHAT BUSINESS I TRADE IN. I AM IN THE BUSINESS OF MURDER. MY STORIES REVOLVE AROUND MURDER MOST FOUL.
EVERY GREAT STORY BEGINS WITH ORIGINS... AT LEAST, AN ORIGIN STORY IS ASSUMED; THIS IS MORE IMPORTANT THAN YOU MIGHT FATHOM RIGHT NOW.
AN AGEING COUPLE DISCOVER THE SMOULDERING REMAINS OF AN EXPIRED METEORITE ON AN ISOLATED KANSAS COUNTRY LANE. THE UNEARTHED REMAINS REVEAL AN EXTRATERRESTRIAL INFANT FROM A DEAD WORLD.
A YOUNG FAMILY IS DONE WITH A PLEASANT NIGHT'S ENTERTAINMENT. BUT THE NIGHT'S PLEASANTRIES ARE CUT SHORT BY A WELL-PLACED PREDATOR. A FATHER AND MOTHER WOULD BE DEAD, A LONE CHILD WOULD BE LEFT AS SOLE, UNRELIABLE WITNESS.
SUPERMAN, THE PRINCE OF KRYPTON. BATMAN, THE PRINCE OF GOTHAM. ISRAEL, THE PRINCE OF HEAVEN. THE HERO ORIGIN STORY, HERO IDENTITY AND HERO NAME ARE INDISTINGUISHABLE IN ESSENCE. THEY ARE FORGED IN THE FLAMES AND TORRENT OF CHAOS AND PURPOSE.

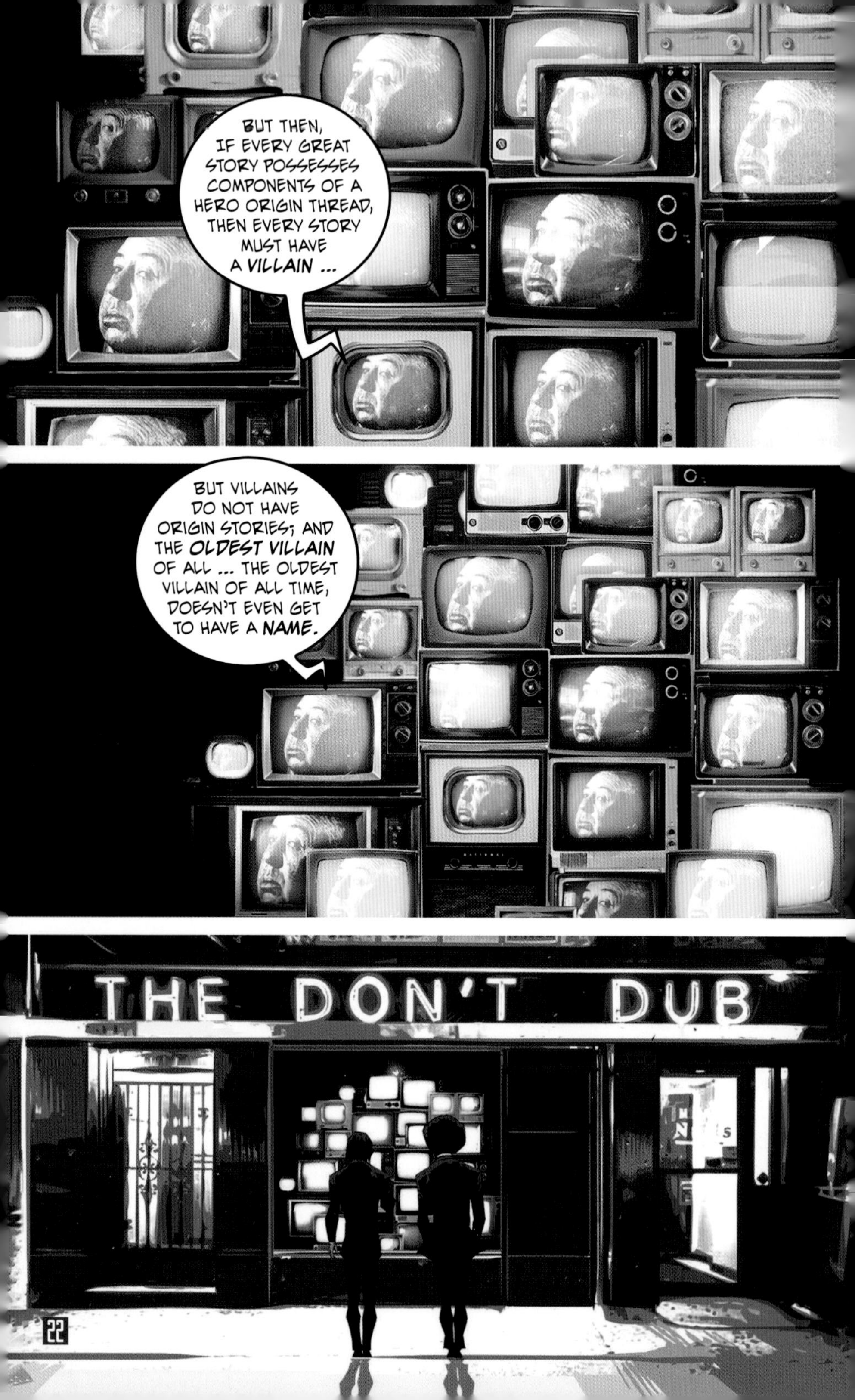
BUT THEN, IF EVERY GREAT STORY POSSESSES COMPONENTS OF A HERO ORIGIN THREAD, THEN EVERY STORY MUST HAVE A VILLAIN ...
BUT VILLAINS DO NOT HAVE ORIGIN STORIES; AND THE OLDEST VILLAIN OF ALL ... THE OLDEST VILLAIN OF ALL TIME, DOESN'T EVEN GET TO HAVE A NAME.
THE DON'T DUB

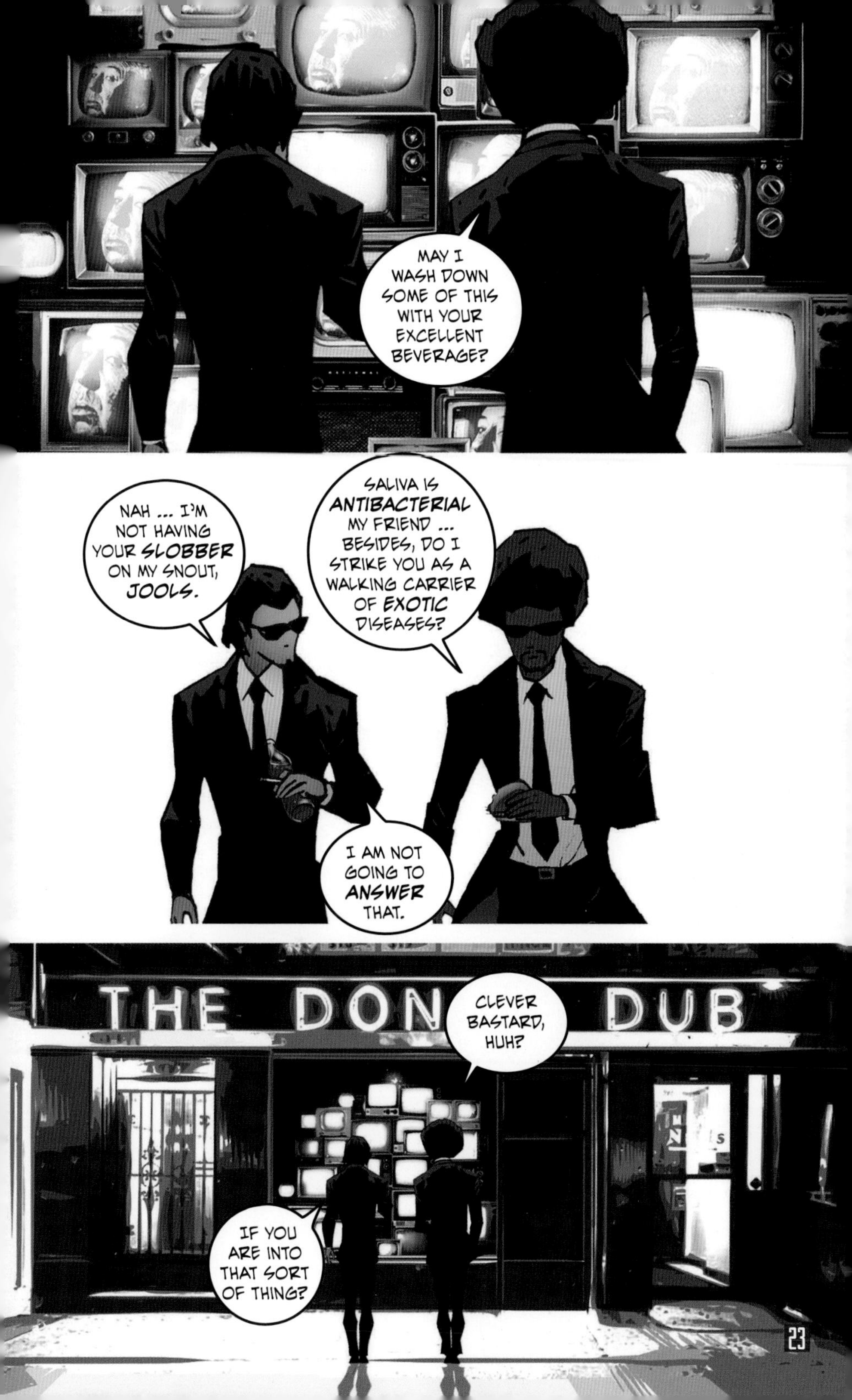
MAY I WASH DOWN SOME OF THIS WITH YOUR EXCELLENT BEVERAGE?
NAH ... I'M NOT HAVING YOUR SLOBBER ON MY SNOUT, JOOLS.
SALIVA IS ANTIBACTERIAL MY FRIEND ... BESIDES, DO I STRIKE YOU AS A WALKING CARRIER OF EXOTIC DISEASES?
I AM NOT GOING TO ANSWER THAT.
THE DON DUB
CLEVER BASTARD, HUH?
IF YOU ARE INTO THAT SORT OF THING?

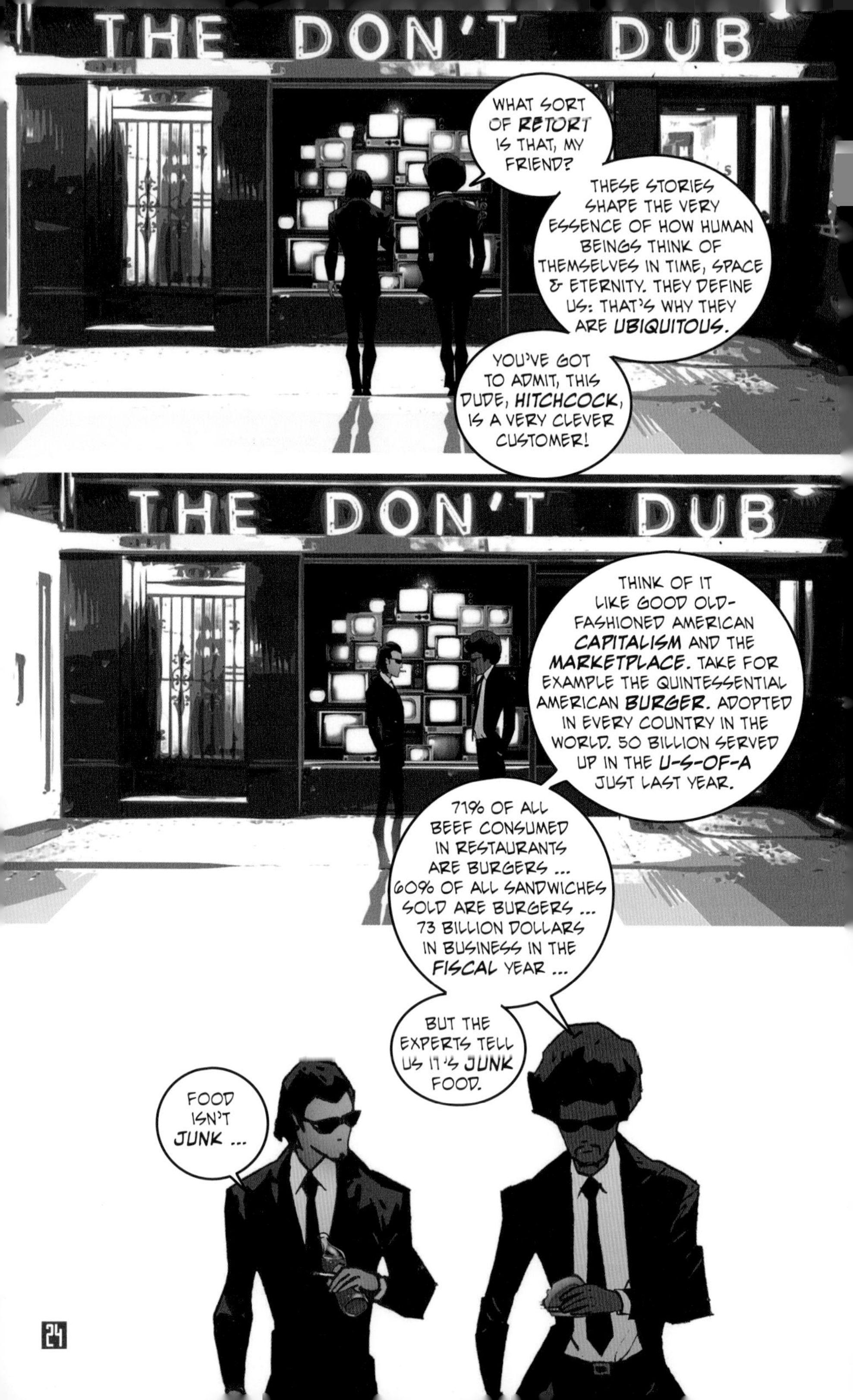
THE DON'T DUB
WHAT SORT OF RETORT IS THAT, MY FRIEND?
THESE STORIES SHAPE THE VERY ESSENCE OF HOW HUMAN BEINGS THINK OF THEMSELVES IN TIME, SPACE & ETERNITY. THEY DEFINE US: THAT'S WHY THEY ARE UBIQUITOUS.
YOU'VE GOT TO ADMIT, THIS DUDE, HITCHCOCK, IS A VERY CLEVER CUSTOMER!
THE DON'T DUB
THINK OF IT LIKE GOOD OLD-FASHIONED AMERICAN CAPITALISM AND THE MARKETPLACE. TAKE FOR EXAMPLE THE QUINTESSENTIAL AMERICAN BURGER. ADOPTED IN EVERY COUNTRY IN THE WORLD. 50 BILLION SERVED UP IN THE U-S-OF-A JUST LAST YEAR.
71% OF ALL BEEF CONSUMED IN RESTAURANTS ARE BURGERS ... 60% OF ALL SANDWICHES SOLD ARE BURGERS ... 73 BILLION DOLLARS IN BUSINESS IN THE FISCAL YEAR ...
BUT THE EXPERTS TELL US IT'S JUNK FOOD.
FOOD ISN'T JUNK ...

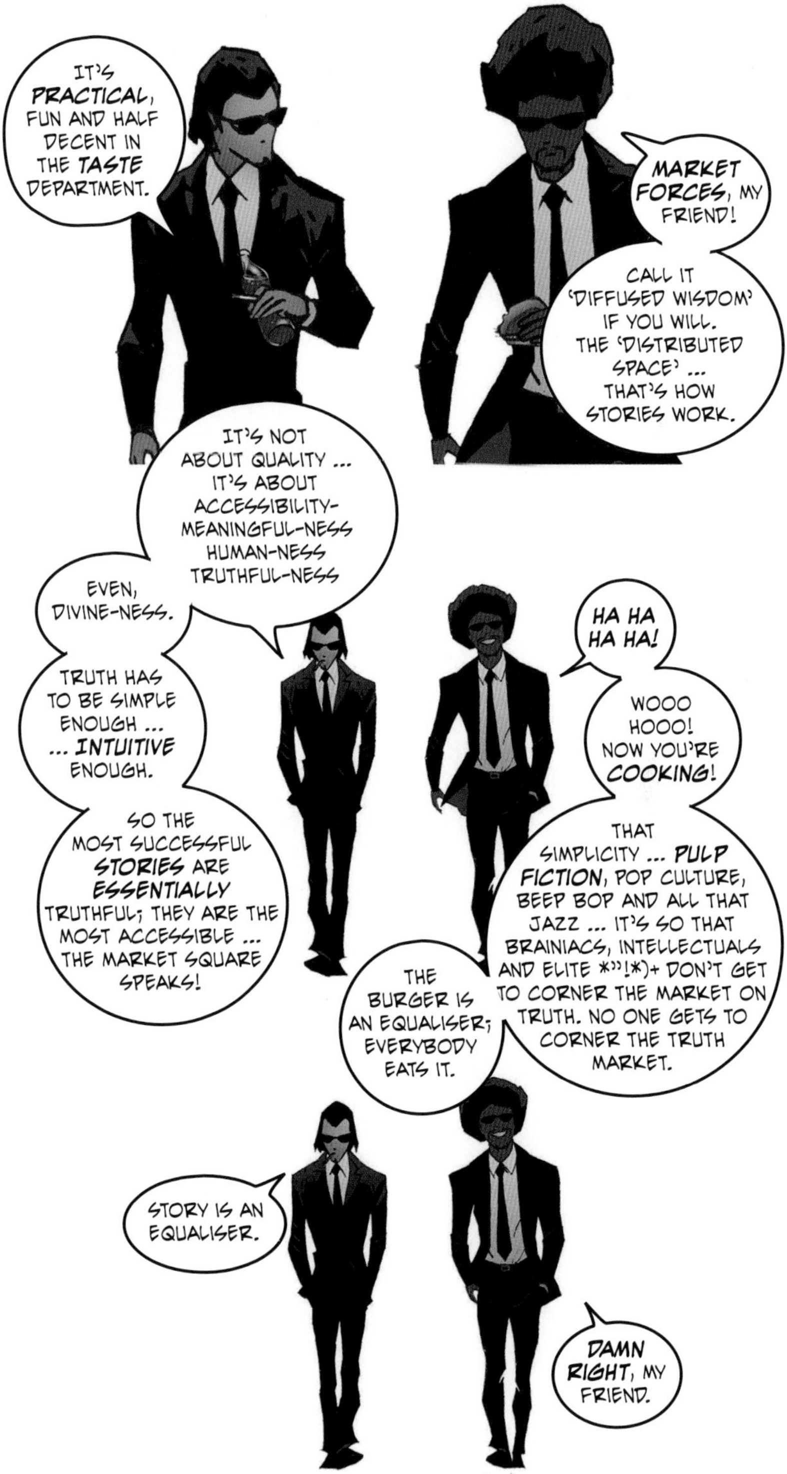
IT'S PRACTICAL, FUN AND HALF DECENT IN THE TASTE DEPARTMENT.
MARKET FORCES, MY FRIEND!
CALL IT 'DIFFUSED WISDOM' IF YOU WILL. THE 'DISTRIBUTED SPACE' ... THAT'S HOW STORIES WORK.
IT'S NOT ABOUT QUALITY ... IT'S ABOUT ACCESSIBILITY-MEANINGFUL-NESS HUMAN-NESS TRUTHFUL-NESS
EVEN, DIVINE-NESS.
HA HA HA HA!
TRUTH HAS TO BE SIMPLE ENOUGH ... ... INTUITIVE ENOUGH.
WOOO HOOO! NOW YOU'RE COOKING!
SO THE MOST SUCCESSFUL STORIES ARE ESSENTIALLY TRUTHFUL; THEY ARE THE MOST ACCESSIBLE ... THE MARKET SQUARE SPEAKS!
THAT SIMPLICITY ... PULP FICTION, POP CULTURE, BEEP BOP AND ALL THAT JAZZ ... IT'S SO THAT BRAINIACS, INTELLECTUALS AND ELITE *"!*)+ DON'T GET TO CORNER THE MARKET ON TRUTH. NO ONE GETS TO CORNER THE TRUTH MARKET.
THE BURGER IS AN EQUALISER; EVERYBODY EATS IT.
STORY IS AN EQUALISER.
DAMN RIGHT, MY FRIEND.

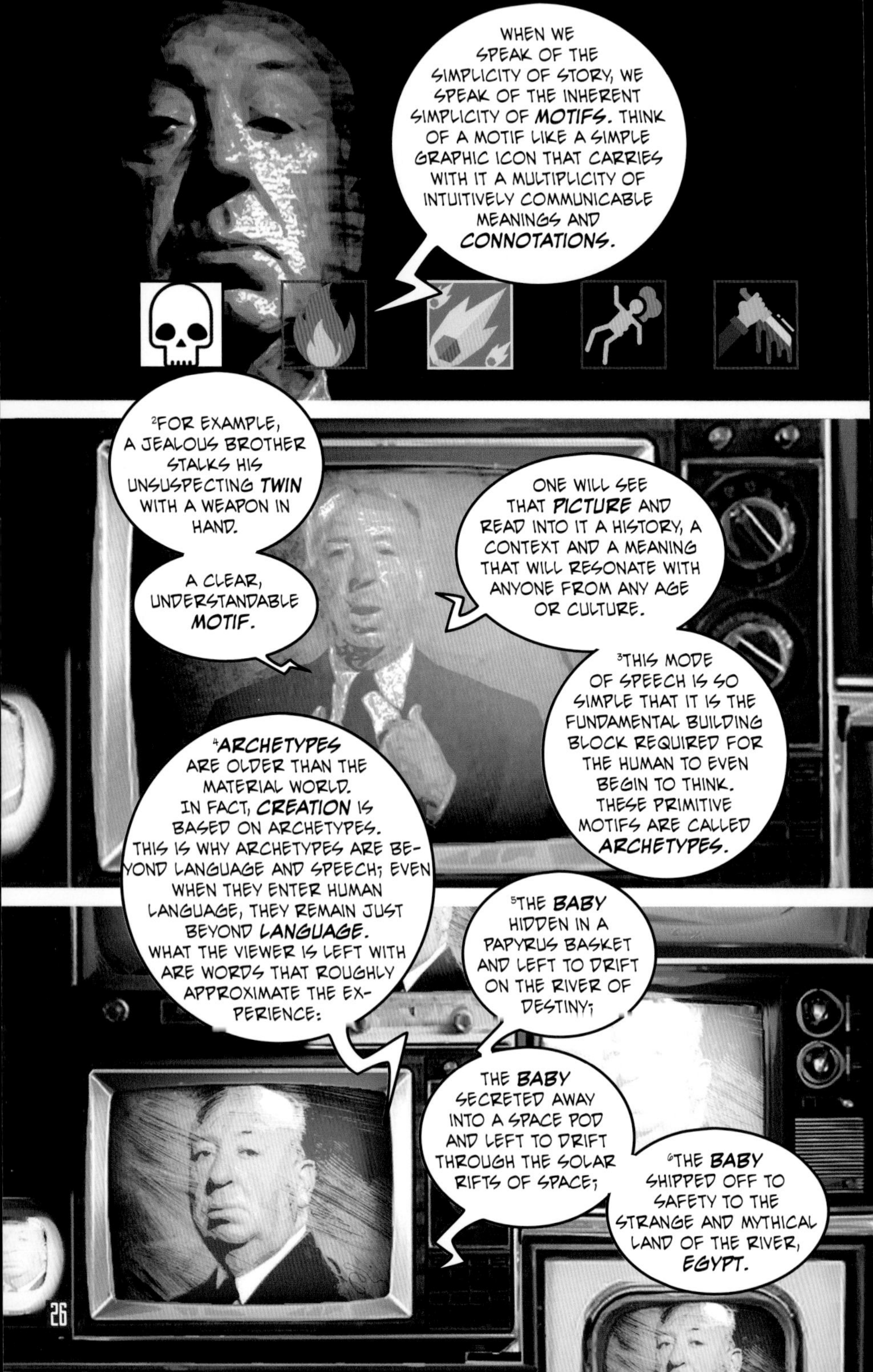
WHEN WE SPEAK OF THE SIMPLICITY OF STORY, WE SPEAK OF THE INHERENT SIMPLICITY OF **MOTIFS.** THINK OF A MOTIF LIKE A SIMPLE GRAPHIC ICON THAT CARRIES WITH IT A MULTIPLICITY OF INTUITIVELY COMMUNICABLE MEANINGS AND **CONNOTATIONS.**
[2]FOR EXAMPLE, A JEALOUS BROTHER STALKS HIS UNSUSPECTING **TWIN** WITH A WEAPON IN HAND.
A CLEAR, UNDERSTANDABLE **MOTIF.**
ONE WILL SEE THAT **PICTURE** AND READ INTO IT A HISTORY, A CONTEXT AND A MEANING THAT WILL RESONATE WITH ANYONE FROM ANY AGE OR CULTURE.
[3]THIS MODE OF SPEECH IS SO SIMPLE THAT IT IS THE FUNDAMENTAL BUILDING BLOCK REQUIRED FOR THE HUMAN TO EVEN BEGIN TO THINK. THESE PRIMITIVE MOTIFS ARE CALLED **ARCHETYPES.**
[4]**ARCHETYPES** ARE OLDER THAN THE MATERIAL WORLD. IN FACT, **CREATION** IS BASED ON ARCHETYPES. THIS IS WHY ARCHETYPES ARE BEYOND LANGUAGE AND SPEECH; EVEN WHEN THEY ENTER HUMAN LANGUAGE, THEY REMAIN JUST BEYOND **LANGUAGE.** WHAT THE VIEWER IS LEFT WITH ARE WORDS THAT ROUGHLY APPROXIMATE THE EXPERIENCE:
[5]THE **BABY** HIDDEN IN A PAPYRUS BASKET AND LEFT TO DRIFT ON THE RIVER OF DESTINY;
THE **BABY** SECRETED AWAY INTO A SPACE POD AND LEFT TO DRIFT THROUGH THE SOLAR RIFTS OF SPACE;
[6]THE **BABY** SHIPPED OFF TO SAFETY TO THE STRANGE AND MYTHICAL LAND OF THE RIVER, **EGYPT.**

Our ability to understand these motifs surpasses our ability to speak about these motifs. We understand the image of a man poised to strike with a blade in hand against the image of a bathing woman in a shower, on conscious and unconscious levels. That's beyond anything you can say on the subject. Terror, angst and awe are just some of the experiences native to the most primitive parts of our being that stubbornly remain beyond our capacity to express in words.

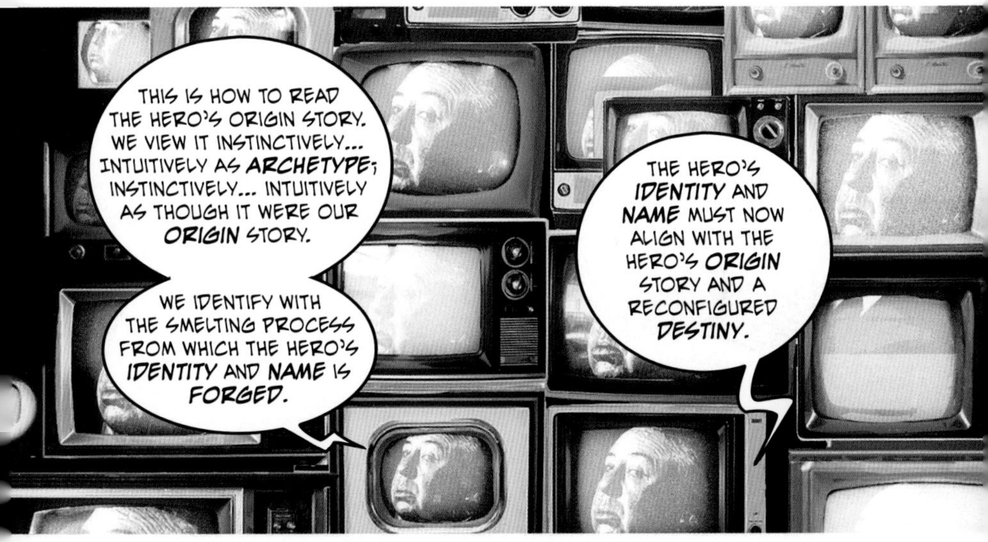
THIS IS HOW TO READ THE HERO'S ORIGIN STORY. WE VIEW IT INSTINCTIVELY... INTUITIVELY AS ARCHETYPE; INSTINCTIVELY... INTUITIVELY AS THOUGH IT WERE OUR ORIGIN STORY.
WE IDENTIFY WITH THE SMELTING PROCESS FROM WHICH THE HERO'S IDENTITY AND NAME IS FORGED.
THE HERO'S IDENTITY AND NAME MUST NOW ALIGN WITH THE HERO'S ORIGIN STORY AND A RECONFIGURED DESTINY.

Abram must become Abraham
Clark Kent must become Superman
Jacob must become Israel

One identity is revealed; the other is concealed.

But this is just one side of the hero paradigm; the story of identity is about to get weirder and much stranger than you can possibly imagine.

REFERENCES

1.   The mark of Cain. Genesis 4:15.

2.   Genesis 4:8.

3.   Serotonergically speaking: these archetypes create hierarchies of meaning. These are meta-verbal orders – they imply ways of thinking that are beyond speech. The old school promised us that we needed words in order to think, but they were wrong. Babies are clearly capable of thought months before they can begin to recognise words. The latest research is demonstrating a *poetic-soma-psycho* dynamic when it comes to consciousness. It's just a little more complex than materialists would have you believe. Closer to magic than mere science. See John Vervaeke's discussion with Jonathan Pageau: *https://www.youtube.com/watch?v=2PGglfl5j_I   https://www.youtube.com/watch?v=5enaol6dGWU*

4.   Genesis 1:2-4, John 1:1-5, Proverbs 8:23-29 (*archetype* is a characteristic of *wisdom*; She is a UNIVERSALS phenomenon). *Wisdom* works in conjunction with its lower sphere companion, '*Understanding*'. *Wisdom* is pre-verbal/super-verbal ... that is to say, 'magic'. *Understanding*, on the other hand, is a PARTICULARS phenomenon. It is verbal ... that is to say, 'science'. We will see this dynamic migrate in the superhero matrix.

5.   Exodus 2:3, Morrison, G. 2011. *Supergods: Our World in the Age of the Superhero.* United Kingdom, Jonathan Cape Limited, p. 16.

6.   Matthew 2:13-15.

GATE ONE

THE CALL

METROPOLIS

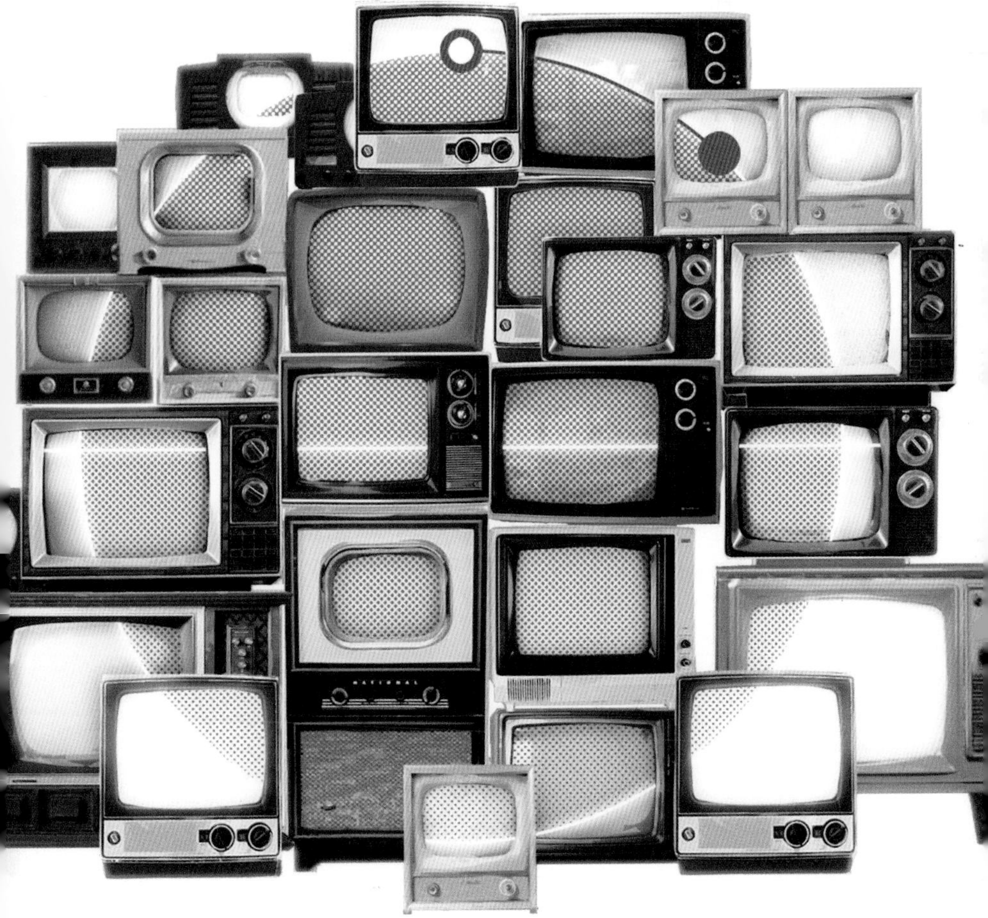

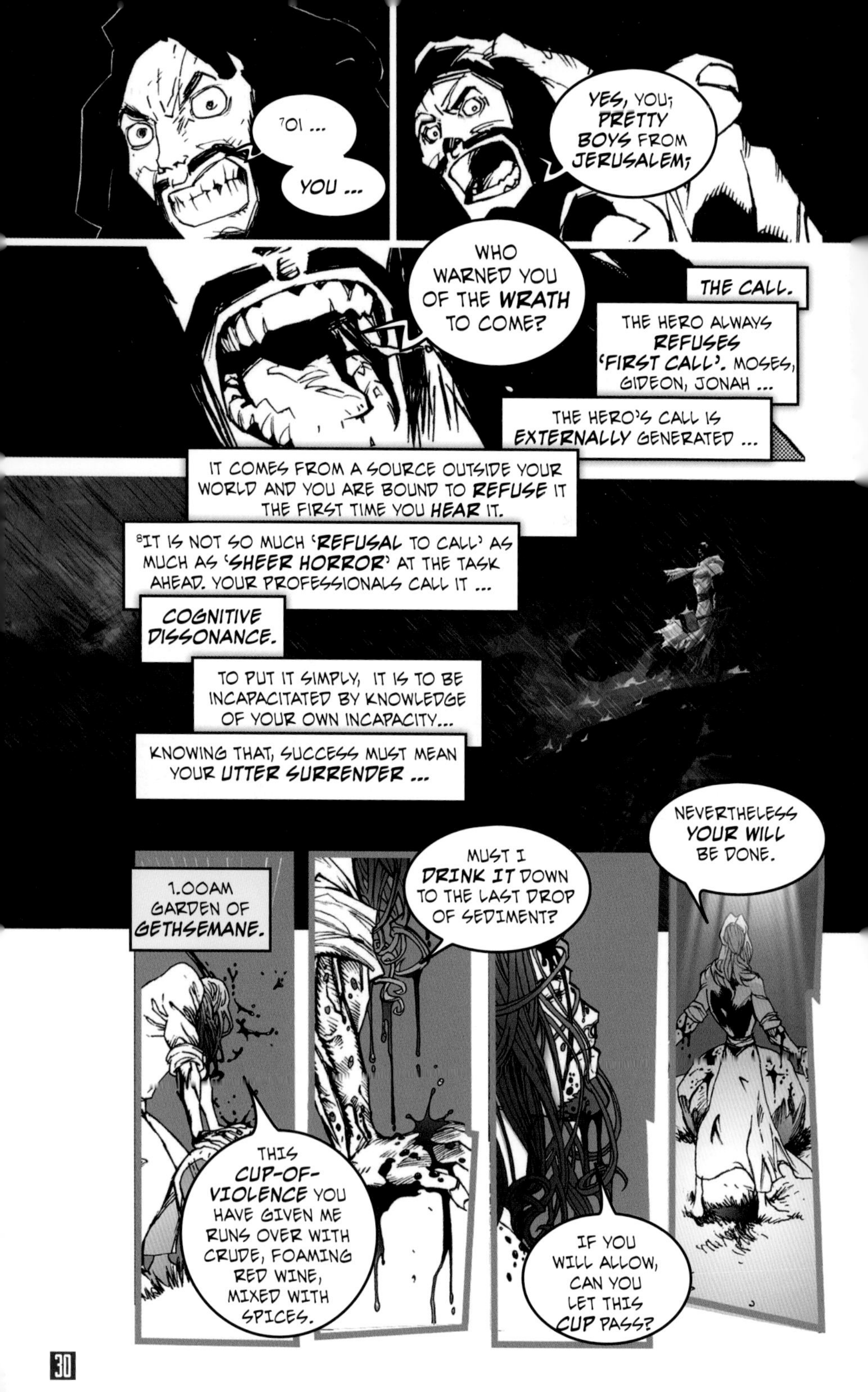

[7]OI ...
YOU ...
YES, YOU; PRETTY BOYS FROM JERUSALEM;
WHO WARNED YOU OF THE WRATH TO COME?
THE CALL.
THE HERO ALWAYS REFUSES 'FIRST CALL'. MOSES, GIDEON, JONAH ...
THE HERO'S CALL IS EXTERNALLY GENERATED ...
IT COMES FROM A SOURCE OUTSIDE YOUR WORLD AND YOU ARE BOUND TO REFUSE IT THE FIRST TIME YOU HEAR IT.
[8]IT IS NOT SO MUCH 'REFUSAL TO CALL' AS MUCH AS 'SHEER HORROR' AT THE TASK AHEAD. YOUR PROFESSIONALS CALL IT ...
COGNITIVE DISSONANCE.
TO PUT IT SIMPLY, IT IS TO BE INCAPACITATED BY KNOWLEDGE OF YOUR OWN INCAPACITY...
KNOWING THAT, SUCCESS MUST MEAN YOUR UTTER SURRENDER ...
1.00AM GARDEN OF GETHSEMANE.
THIS CUP-OF-VIOLENCE YOU HAVE GIVEN ME RUNS OVER WITH CRUDE, FOAMING RED WINE, MIXED WITH SPICES.
MUST I DRINK IT DOWN TO THE LAST DROP OF SEDIMENT?
IF YOU WILL ALLOW, CAN YOU LET THIS CUP PASS?
NEVERTHELESS YOUR WILL BE DONE.

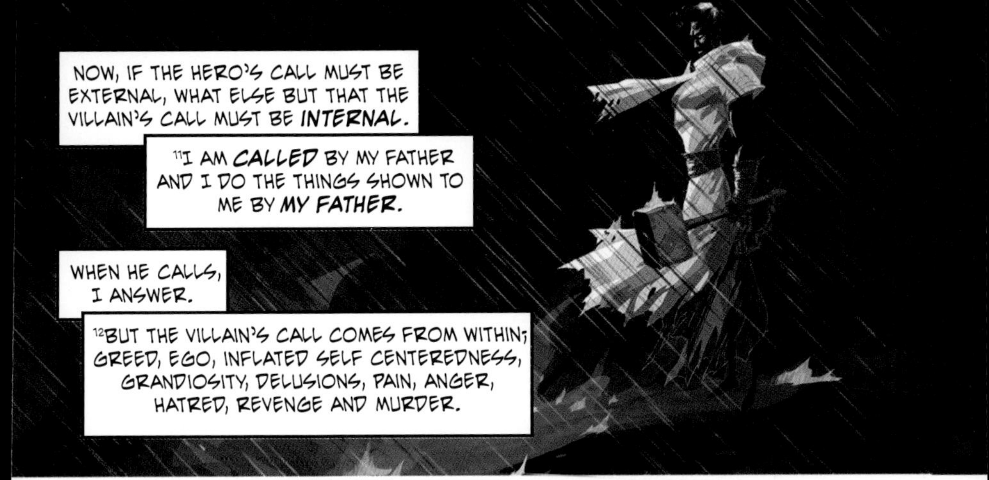
NOW, IF THE HERO'S CALL MUST BE EXTERNAL, WHAT ELSE BUT THAT THE VILLAIN'S CALL MUST BE **INTERNAL**.
[11]I AM ***CALLED*** BY MY FATHER AND I DO THE THINGS SHOWN TO ME BY ***MY FATHER***.
WHEN HE CALLS, I ANSWER.
[12]BUT THE VILLAIN'S CALL COMES FROM WITHIN; GREED, EGO, INFLATED SELF CENTEREDNESS, GRANDIOSITY, DELUSIONS, PAIN, ANGER, HATRED, REVENGE AND MURDER.

[13]THERE IS NO HORROR AT THE TASK AHEAD OF ABSALOM BECAUSE THERE IS NO SACRIFICE ON THE ROAD AHEAD. ABSALOM'S CALL IS ENTIRELY GENERATED FROM WITHIN AND EVERY SACRIFICE REQUIRED WOULD BE PAID BY JERUSALEM. THE CURRENT GOING RATE: BLOOD; TEARS ARE ALSO ACCEPTABLE.

WHAT WAS IT I SAID IN PROPHET SAMUEL'S SCROLL? [14]"THIS IS THE WAY THE KIND OF KING YOU'RE TALKING ABOUT OPERATES. HE'LL TAKE YOUR SONS AND MAKE SOLDIERS OF THEM — CHARIOTRY, CAVALRY, INFANTRY, REGIMENTED IN BATTALIONS AND SQUADRONS. HE'LL PUT SOME TO FORCED LABOR ON HIS FARMS, PLOWING AND HARVESTING, AND OTHERS TO MAKING EITHER WEAPONS OF WAR OR CHARIOTS IN WHICH HE CAN RIDE IN LUXURY. HE'LL PUT YOUR DAUGHTERS TO WORK AS BEAUTICIANS AND WAITRESSES AND COOKS. HE'LL CONSCRIPT YOUR BEST FIELDS, VINEYARDS, AND ORCHARDS AND HAND THEM OVER TO HIS SPECIAL FRIENDS. HE'LL TAX YOUR HARVESTS AND VINTAGE TO SUPPORT HIS EXTENSIVE BUREAUCRACY. YOUR PRIZE WORKERS AND BEST ANIMALS HE'LL TAKE FOR HIS OWN USE. HE'LL LAY A TAX ON YOUR FLOCKS AND YOU'LL END UP NO BETTER THAN SLAVES."

THERE IS NO COGNITIVE DISSONANCE WITHIN THE VILLAIN'S SPIRITUAL FRAMEWORK BECAUSE THE VILLAIN IS NOT REQUIRED TO SACRIFICE ANYTHING; ANY SACRIFICING WILL BE DONE BY HIS UNSUSPECTING VICTIMS AND OPPONENTS — HE IS A [15]WATERLESS CLOUD ... [16]A WANDERING STAR ...

THE HERO PURSUES REDEMPTION OF ALL UNTO HIS DEATH; THE VILLAIN WILL PURSUE HIS OWN AGENDA UNTO YOUR OWN DEATH. UNLIKE THE HERO WHO GIVES UP HIS LIFE FOR HIS WOMAN, ABSALOM WOULD RAPE JERUSALEM... THE RAPE AND DESTRUCTION OF HIS BEA UTIFUL SISTER, TAMAR, ONLY A PASSING COMPONENT IN HIS SCHEME TO USURP HIS BROTHER'S THRONE.

TAMAR ... OH TAMAR.

THE VILLAIN HAS AN AGENDA WITHOUT A MISSION, A MISSION WITHOUT A CAUSE, A CAUSE WITHOUT A MEANING, A MEANING FABRICATED ENTIRELY IN HIS DELUDED MIND.

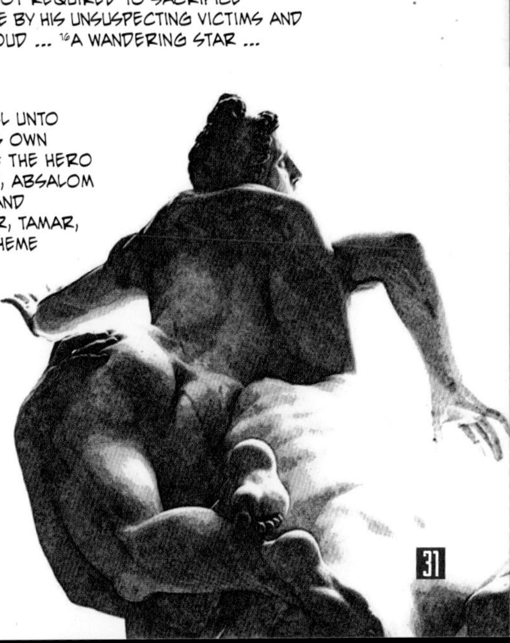

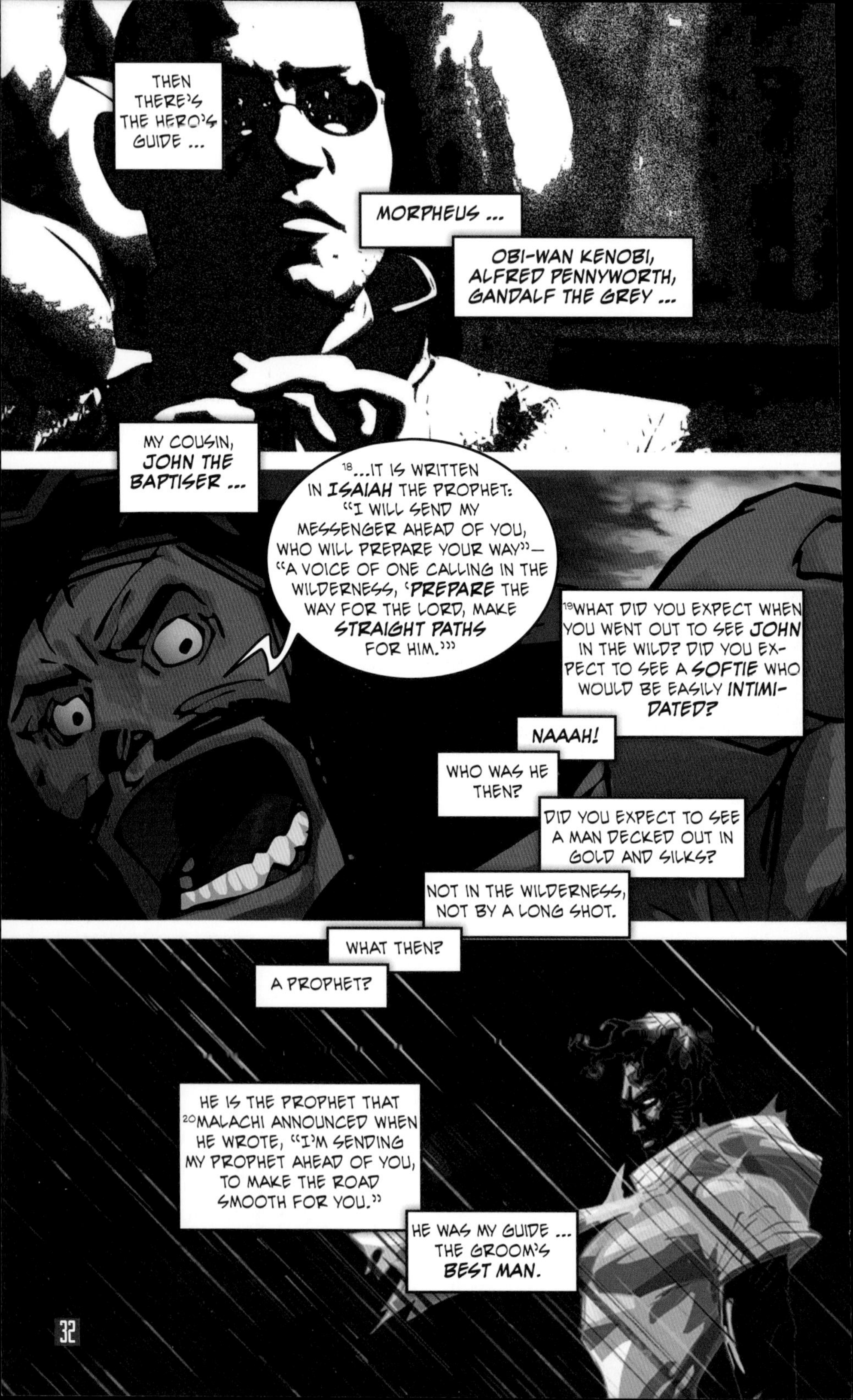
THEN THERE'S THE HERO'S GUIDE ...
MORPHEUS ...
OBI-WAN KENOBI, ALFRED PENNYWORTH, GANDALF THE GREY ...
MY COUSIN, JOHN THE BAPTISER ...
18...IT IS WRITTEN IN ISAIAH THE PROPHET: "I WILL SEND MY MESSENGER AHEAD OF YOU, WHO WILL PREPARE YOUR WAY"— "A VOICE OF ONE CALLING IN THE WILDERNESS, 'PREPARE THE WAY FOR THE LORD, MAKE STRAIGHT PATHS FOR HIM.'"
19WHAT DID YOU EXPECT WHEN YOU WENT OUT TO SEE JOHN IN THE WILD? DID YOU EXPECT TO SEE A SOFTIE WHO WOULD BE EASILY INTIMIDATED?
NAAAH!
WHO WAS HE THEN?
DID YOU EXPECT TO SEE A MAN DECKED OUT IN GOLD AND SILKS?
NOT IN THE WILDERNESS, NOT BY A LONG SHOT.
WHAT THEN?
A PROPHET?
HE IS THE PROPHET THAT 20MALACHI ANNOUNCED WHEN HE WROTE, "I'M SENDING MY PROPHET AHEAD OF YOU, TO MAKE THE ROAD SMOOTH FOR YOU."
HE WAS MY GUIDE ... THE GROOM'S BEST MAN.

²¹DIDN'T YOU UNDERSTAND MY MIRACLE AT *THE WEDDING* AT KANA?

²²YOU YOURSELVES ARE MY WITNESSES THAT I SAID, "I AM NOT THE CHRIST," BUT, "I HAVE BEEN SENT AHEAD OF HIM." HE WHO HAS THE *BRIDE* IS THE *GROOM*; BUT THE FRIEND OF THE GROOM, WHO STANDS AND LISTENS TO HIM, REJOICES GREATLY BECAUSE OF THE GROOM'S VOICE. SO THIS JOY OF MINE HAS BEEN MADE FULL. HE MUST *INCREASE*, BUT I MUST *DECREASE*.

THE FIRST DAYS WERE WHAT YOUR *THEOLOGIANS* CALL THE 'SPRING PERIOD' OF MY MINISTRY; THE WEDDING AT KANA, FEEDING OF THE FIVE THOUSAND AND THE VIRTUAL CORONATION AFTER THAT.

IT WAS LIKE HOW WE FLIRTED BACK IN THE DAY IN THE DESERT; WHEN WE WERE LIKE *BEDOUIN NOMADS*; MAKING TENT – BREAKING TENT. WE DIDN'T HAVE A LOT BACK THEN, BUT WE WERE HAPPY ... HOPEFUL FOR THE FUTURE.

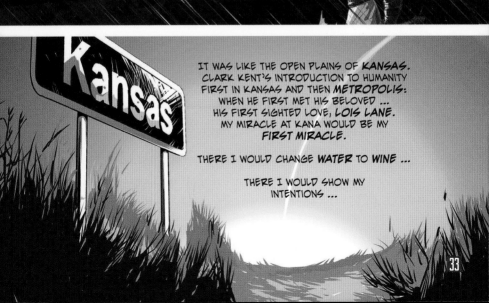

IT WAS LIKE THE OPEN PLAINS OF *KANSAS.* CLARK KENT'S INTRODUCTION TO HUMANITY FIRST IN KANSAS AND THEN *METROPOLIS:* WHEN HE FIRST MET HIS BELOVED ... HIS FIRST SIGHTED LOVE, *LOIS LANE.* MY MIRACLE AT KANA WOULD BE MY *FIRST MIRACLE.*

THERE I WOULD CHANGE *WATER* TO *WINE* ...

THERE I WOULD SHOW MY INTENTIONS ...

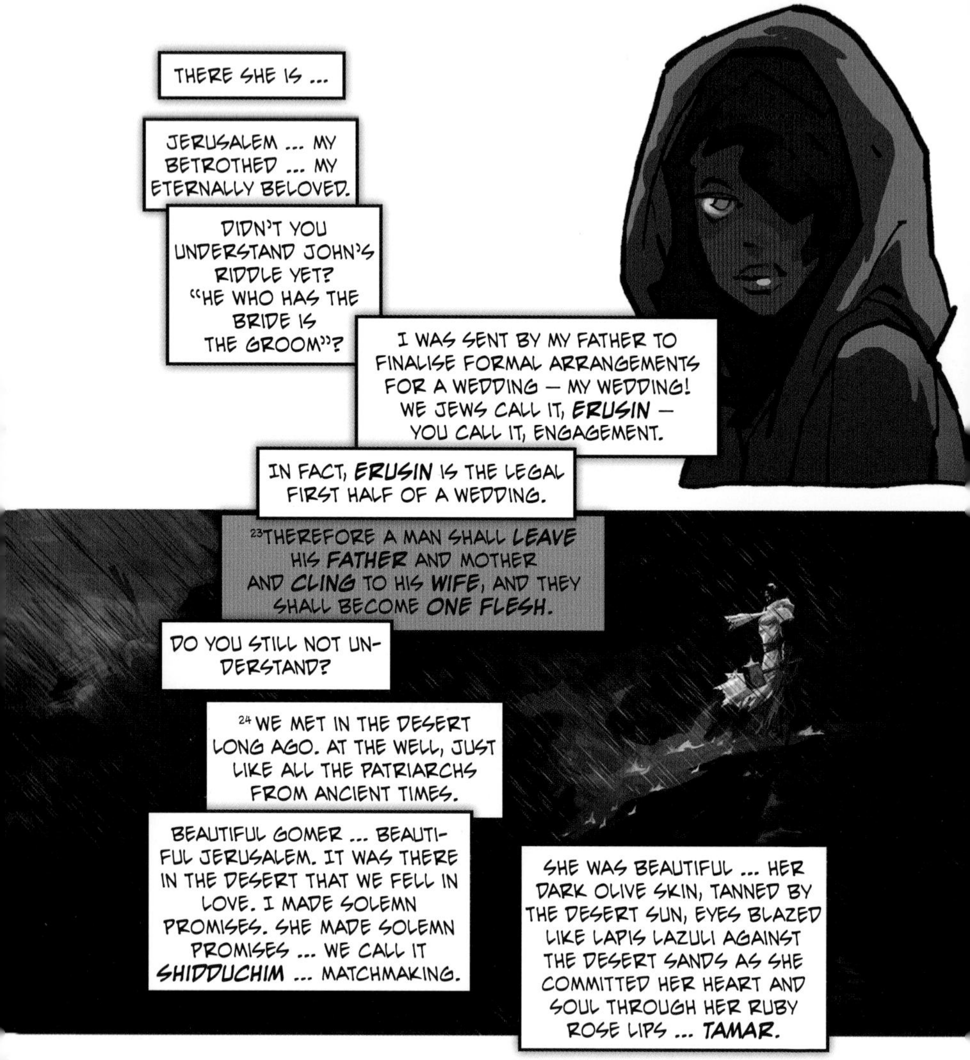
THERE SHE IS ...
JERUSALEM ... MY BETROTHED ... MY ETERNALLY BELOVED.
DIDN'T YOU UNDERSTAND JOHN'S RIDDLE YET? "HE WHO HAS THE BRIDE IS THE GROOM"?
I WAS SENT BY MY FATHER TO FINALISE FORMAL ARRANGEMENTS FOR A WEDDING — MY WEDDING! WE JEWS CALL IT, *ERUSIN* — YOU CALL IT, ENGAGEMENT.
IN FACT, *ERUSIN* IS THE LEGAL FIRST HALF OF A WEDDING.
23 THEREFORE A MAN SHALL *LEAVE* HIS *FATHER* AND MOTHER AND *CLING* TO HIS *WIFE*, AND THEY SHALL BECOME *ONE FLESH*.
DO YOU STILL NOT UNDERSTAND?
24 WE MET IN THE DESERT LONG AGO. AT THE WELL, JUST LIKE ALL THE PATRIARCHS FROM ANCIENT TIMES.
BEAUTIFUL GOMER ... BEAUTIFUL JERUSALEM. IT WAS THERE IN THE DESERT THAT WE FELL IN LOVE. I MADE SOLEMN PROMISES. SHE MADE SOLEMN PROMISES ... WE CALL IT *SHIDDUCHIM* ... MATCHMAKING.
SHE WAS BEAUTIFUL ... HER DARK OLIVE SKIN, TANNED BY THE DESERT SUN, EYES BLAZED LIKE LAPIS LAZULI AGAINST THE DESERT SANDS AS SHE COMMITTED HER HEART AND SOUL THROUGH HER RUBY ROSE LIPS ... *TAMAR*.

The match was made. My father had chosen well. She was perfect. I would return with the *mohar* — a dowry upon which the engagement would commence.

But then ... she broke my heart. Ba'al and Astaroth would ravish her and Absalom would rape her. She would find comfort in the arms of strangers, looters and murderers.

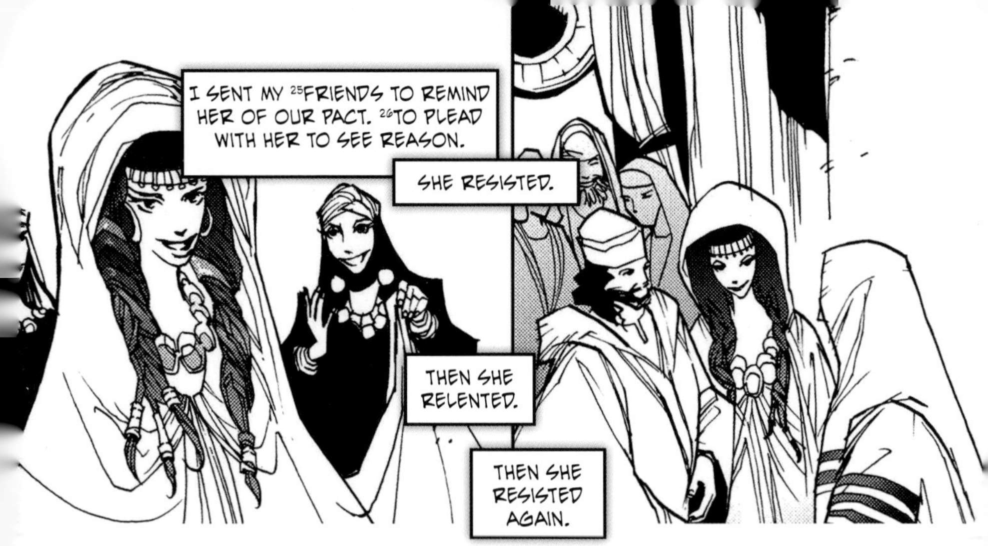
I SENT MY [25]FRIENDS TO REMIND HER OF OUR PACT. [26]TO PLEAD WITH HER TO SEE REASON.
SHE RESISTED.
THEN SHE RELENTED.
THEN SHE RESISTED AGAIN.

And then [27]relented.

So I sent my [28] best man ahead of my arrival for the exchange of engagement contracts. We call it *Ketubah*. It is a legal document that makes it as good as a wedding. But it is not ceremonial … that comes after what we call a gap year. Wedding dresses are made, the bride is being trained, messages are passed between love couples …

During this gap year, I would have returned to my father.

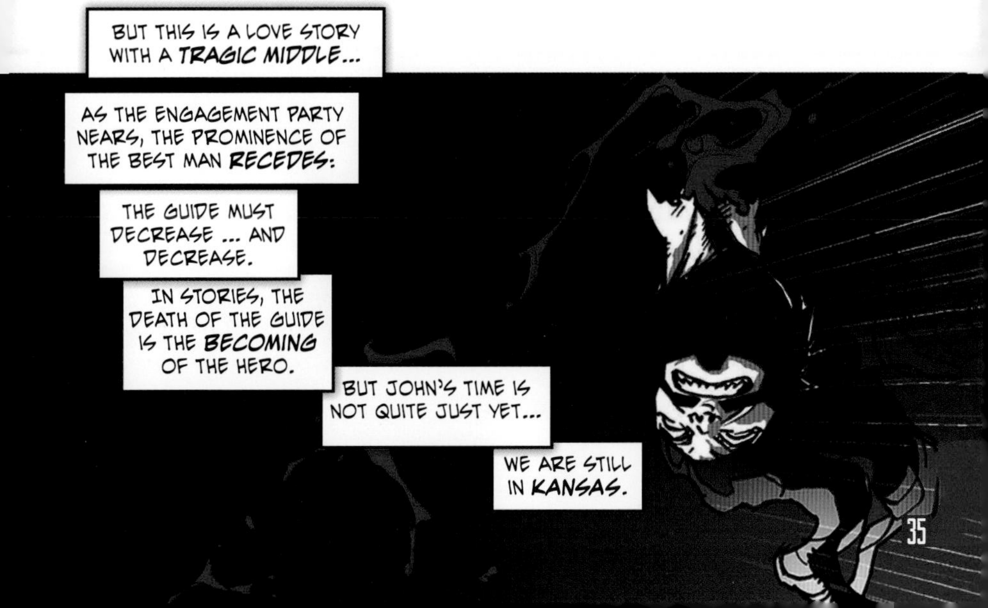
BUT THIS IS A LOVE STORY WITH A ***TRAGIC MIDDLE***...
AS THE ENGAGEMENT PARTY NEARS, THE PROMINENCE OF THE BEST MAN ***RECEDES***:
THE GUIDE MUST DECREASE ... AND DECREASE.
IN STORIES, THE DEATH OF THE GUIDE IS THE ***BECOMING*** OF THE HERO.
BUT JOHN'S TIME IS NOT QUITE JUST YET...
WE ARE STILL IN ***KANSAS***.

REFERENCES

7.   Dramatised: Matthew 3:7.

8.   Luke 22:42.

9.   Revelation 5:4-5. Isaiah 6:5.

10. Siku. 2010. *The Manga Jesus*, London: Hodder and Stoughton. p. 225.

11. John 8:28, 12:49, Matthew 15:13. There are 46 'My father' related verses in the gospel of John alone.

12. Matthew 23:15.

13. 2 Samuel 13-19.

14. 1 Samuel 8:11-18 (The Message translation).

15. Jude 1:12-13.

16. Of what use is a wandering star to those who journey at night? A wandering star: reminiscent of warring powers in the second heaven; an active, bitter and committed antagonism against God's kingdom.

17. Amnon was heir to David's throne. He was also rapist of his half sister, Tamar.

18. Mark 1:2, Mal. 3:1, Mark 1:3, Isaiah 40:3.

19. Matthew 11:7-10.

20. Malachi 3:1.

21. John 2:1-11.

22. John 3:25-30.

23. Genesis 2:24.

24. John 4:6-7.

25. Matthew 21:36.

26. Isaiah 1:18 (ASV).

27. Hosea 3:4.

28. John 3:29.

GATE TWO

THE CROSSING

DEPARTURE

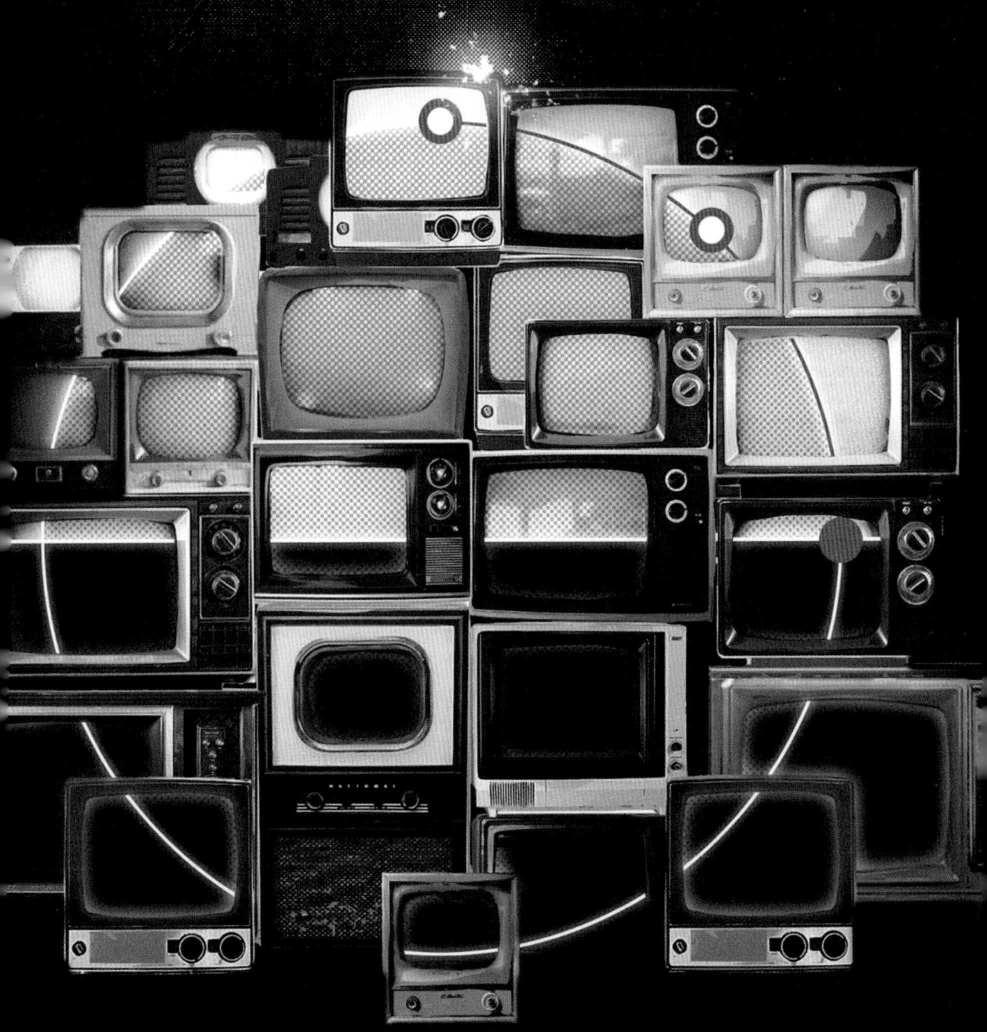

This never happens. I picked up a voicemail message from Paul, the dorm housemaster. You never get a voice message from the dorm housemaster after giving a talk at Eton. But I was expecting one as I listened through my messages after arriving at home. You see, I not only expected a voice message, I expected a rebuke. As I retrieved the message from 'Paul' ... nothing but effusive praise. "The boys loved it!", he shouted! He loved it!

I had given speeches at Eton College at least once every year since 2011 and I was sure this speech, in the fifth consecutive year, would be the last time anyone would let me around polite company.

"They stood around talking about your speech for hours after you left, Siku. That's what we want at Eton; challenging questions and debate!", Paul effused.

Paul is a 'black' South African academic, leading classes at one of the world's most prestigious secondary school institutions whilst pursuing a doctorate degree in Liberation Theology. He and I met at Queen's University in Birmingham where I gave a talk to a group of black theologians about apocalypse genre, narratives, culture and manga. We followed up with our thoughts on theology and narrative and he promptly worked up my first invitation to talk at Eton College. Here was how I was going to repay all that goodwill – by talking about bitches, hoes and a God who sings the blues!

Yep, I was sure this was going to be my last invite. Don't know what made me do a *kamikaze*; trust me, I did try to re-engage some sort of realism but the essence of the narrative kept bringing me back to the same insane conclusion: "You have got to talk about 'bitches'!" So I did.

The speeches were always given in a large auditorium. A mixture of boys from different religions to no religion ... a few hundred in the hall. Engaging, bright, responsive, articulate, polite, poised, funny as usual ... then I said the word!

The boys gasped and then chuckled – you could see some boys exchange glances, "Did he really say what I think he said?" I could almost read the mind of the faculty staff in attendance (Paul) thinking to himself, "Maybe I should have taken a look at Siku's title first?"

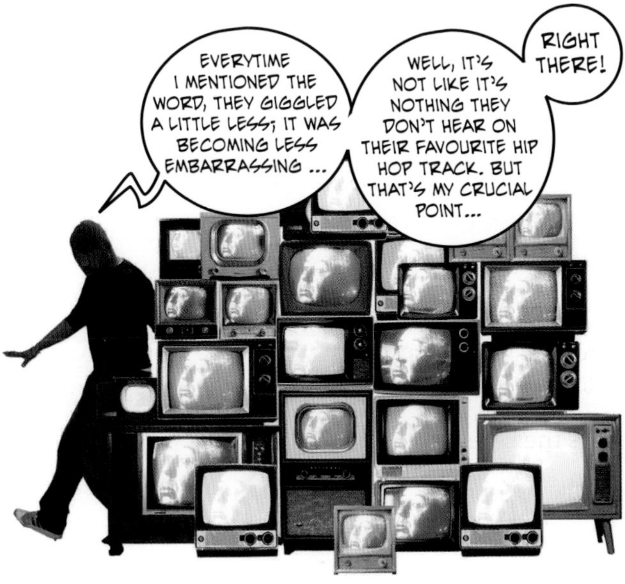
EVERYTIME I MENTIONED THE WORD, THEY GIGGLED A LITTLE LESS; IT WAS BECOMING LESS EMBARRASSING ...
WELL, IT'S NOT LIKE IT'S NOTHING THEY DON'T HEAR ON THEIR FAVOURITE HIP HOP TRACK. BUT THAT'S MY CRUCIAL POINT...
RIGHT THERE!

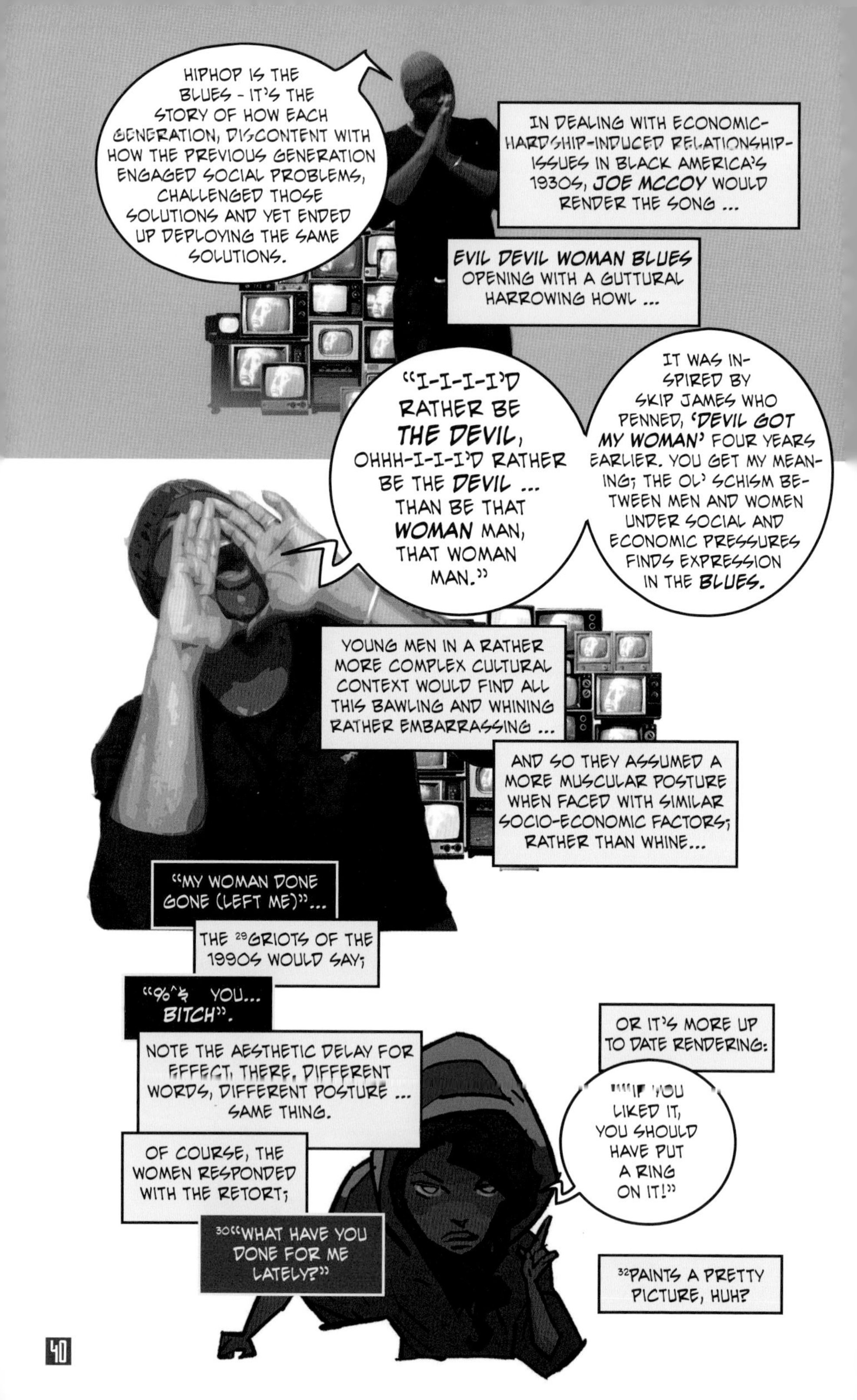
HIPHOP IS THE BLUES - IT'S THE STORY OF HOW EACH GENERATION, DISCONTENT WITH HOW THE PREVIOUS GENERATION ENGAGED SOCIAL PROBLEMS, CHALLENGED THOSE SOLUTIONS AND YET ENDED UP DEPLOYING THE SAME SOLUTIONS.
IN DEALING WITH ECONOMIC-HARDSHIP-INDUCED RELATIONSHIP-ISSUES IN BLACK AMERICA'S 1930S, JOE MCCOY WOULD RENDER THE SONG ...
EVIL DEVIL WOMAN BLUES OPENING WITH A GUTTURAL HARROWING HOWL ...
"I-I-I-I'D RATHER BE THE DEVIL, OHHH-I-I-I'D RATHER BE THE DEVIL ... THAN BE THAT WOMAN MAN, THAT WOMAN MAN."
IT WAS INSPIRED BY SKIP JAMES WHO PENNED, 'DEVIL GOT MY WOMAN' FOUR YEARS EARLIER. YOU GET MY MEANING; THE OL' SCHISM BETWEEN MEN AND WOMEN UNDER SOCIAL AND ECONOMIC PRESSURES FINDS EXPRESSION IN THE BLUES.
YOUNG MEN IN A RATHER MORE COMPLEX CULTURAL CONTEXT WOULD FIND ALL THIS BAWLING AND WHINING RATHER EMBARRASSING ...
AND SO THEY ASSUMED A MORE MUSCULAR POSTURE WHEN FACED WITH SIMILAR SOCIO-ECONOMIC FACTORS; RATHER THAN WHINE...
"MY WOMAN DONE GONE (LEFT ME)"...
THE [29]GRIOTS OF THE 1990S WOULD SAY;
"%^$ YOU... BITCH".
NOTE THE AESTHETIC DELAY FOR EFFECT, THERE. DIFFERENT WORDS, DIFFERENT POSTURE ... SAME THING.
OF COURSE, THE WOMEN RESPONDED WITH THE RETORT;
[30]"WHAT HAVE YOU DONE FOR ME LATELY?"
OR IT'S MORE UP TO DATE RENDERING:
"IF YOU LIKED IT, YOU SHOULD HAVE PUT A RING ON IT!"
[32]PAINTS A PRETTY PICTURE, HUH?

Now, read these texts and weep ... tell me this isn't the blues:

33Ezekiel 23

1-4 God's Message came to me: "Son of man, there were two women, daughters of the same mother. They became whores in Egypt, whores from a young age. Their breasts were fondled, their young bosoms caressed. The older sister was named Oholah, the younger was Oholibah. They were my daughters, and they gave birth to sons and daughters. "Oholah is Samaria and Oholibah is Jerusalem.

5-8 "Oholah started whoring while she was still mine. She lusted after Assyrians as lovers: military men smartly uniformed in blue, ambassadors and governors, good-looking young men mounted on fine horses. Her lust was unrestrained. She was a whore to the Assyrian elite. She compounded her filth with the idols of those to whom she gave herself in lust. She never slowed down. The whoring she began while young in Egypt ...

9-10 "So I left her to her Assyrian lovers, for whom she was so obsessed with lust. They ripped off her clothes, took away her children, and then, the final indignity, killed her.

11"Her sister Oholibah saw all this, but she became even worse than her sister in lust and whoring, if you can believe it. She also went crazy with lust for Assyrians: ambassadors and governors, military men smartly dressed and mounted on fine horses – the Assyrian elite."

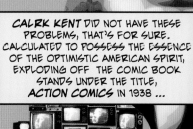

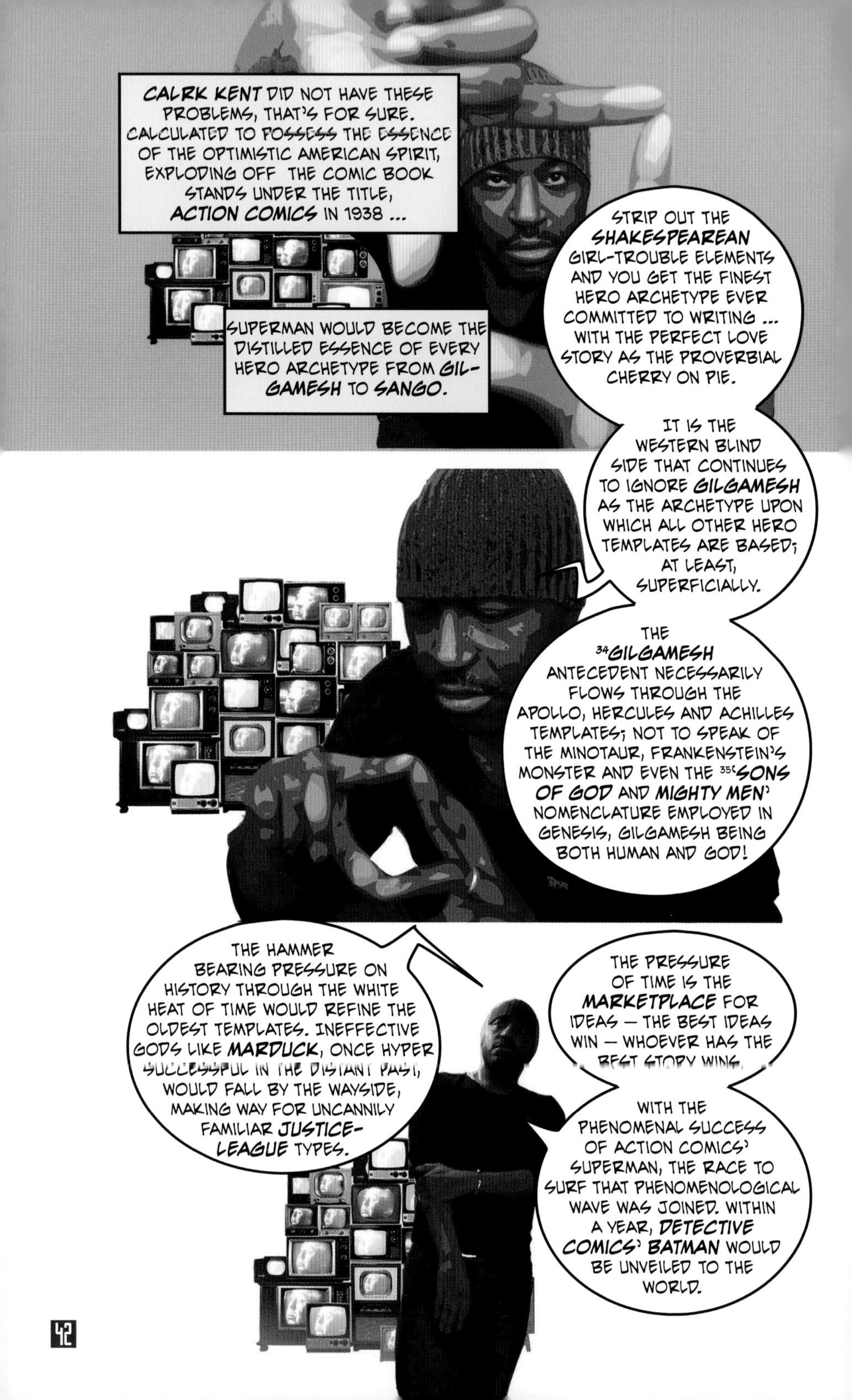

CALRK KENT DID NOT HAVE THESE PROBLEMS, THAT'S FOR SURE. CALCULATED TO POSSESS THE ESSENCE OF THE OPTIMISTIC AMERICAN SPIRIT, EXPLODING OFF THE COMIC BOOK STANDS UNDER THE TITLE, *ACTION COMICS* IN 1938 ...

STRIP OUT THE *SHAKESPEAREAN* GIRL-TROUBLE ELEMENTS AND YOU GET THE FINEST HERO ARCHETYPE EVER COMMITTED TO WRITING ... WITH THE PERFECT LOVE STORY AS THE PROVERBIAL CHERRY ON PIE.

SUPERMAN WOULD BECOME THE DISTILLED ESSENCE OF EVERY HERO ARCHETYPE FROM *GIL-GAMESH* TO *SANGO.*

IT IS THE WESTERN BLIND SIDE THAT CONTINUES TO IGNORE *GILGAMESH* AS THE ARCHETYPE UPON WHICH ALL OTHER HERO TEMPLATES ARE BASED; AT LEAST, SUPERFICIALLY.

THE [34]*GILGAMESH* ANTECEDENT NECESSARILY FLOWS THROUGH THE APOLLO, HERCULES AND ACHILLES TEMPLATES; NOT TO SPEAK OF THE MINOTAUR, FRANKENSTEIN'S MONSTER AND EVEN THE [35]*'SONS OF GOD* AND *MIGHTY MEN'* NOMENCLATURE EMPLOYED IN GENESIS, GILGAMESH BEING BOTH HUMAN AND GOD!

THE HAMMER BEARING PRESSURE ON HISTORY THROUGH THE WHITE HEAT OF TIME WOULD REFINE THE OLDEST TEMPLATES. INEFFECTIVE GODS LIKE *MARDUCK,* ONCE HYPER SUCCESSFUL IN THE DISTANT PAST, WOULD FALL BY THE WAYSIDE, MAKING WAY FOR UNCANNILY FAMILIAR *JUSTICE-LEAGUE* TYPES.

THE PRESSURE OF TIME IS THE *MARKETPLACE* FOR IDEAS — THE BEST IDEAS WIN — WHOEVER HAS THE BEST STORY WINS.

WITH THE PHENOMENAL SUCCESS OF ACTION COMICS' SUPERMAN, THE RACE TO SURF THAT PHENOMENOLOGICAL WAVE WAS JOINED. WITHIN A YEAR, *DETECTIVE COMICS'* BATMAN WOULD BE UNVEILED TO THE WORLD.

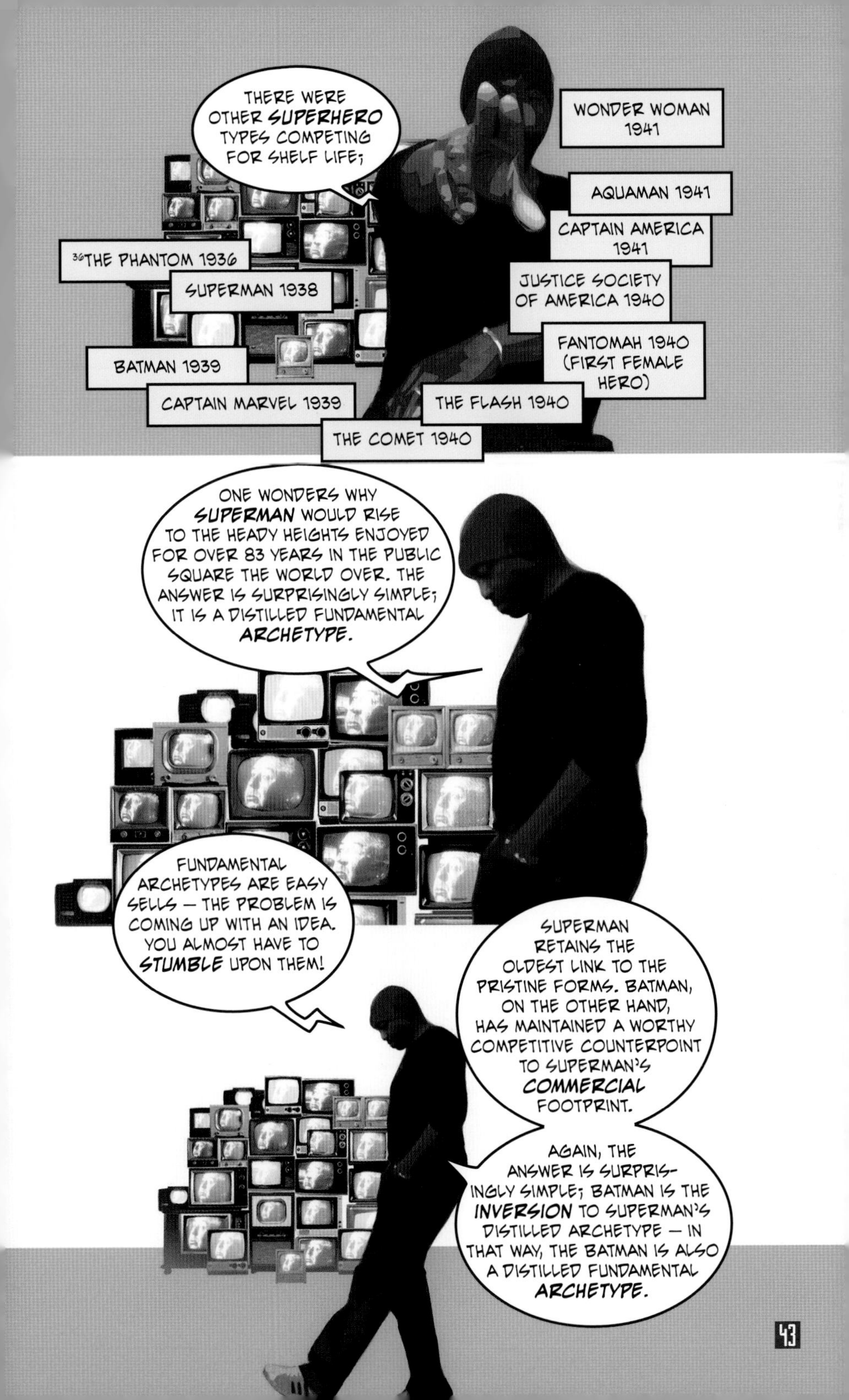

THERE WERE OTHER SUPERHERO TYPES COMPETING FOR SHELF LIFE;
WONDER WOMAN 1941
AQUAMAN 1941
CAPTAIN AMERICA 1941
[36]THE PHANTOM 1936
SUPERMAN 1938
JUSTICE SOCIETY OF AMERICA 1940
BATMAN 1939
FANTOMAH 1940 (FIRST FEMALE HERO)
CAPTAIN MARVEL 1939
THE FLASH 1940
THE COMET 1940
ONE WONDERS WHY SUPERMAN WOULD RISE TO THE HEADY HEIGHTS ENJOYED FOR OVER 83 YEARS IN THE PUBLIC SQUARE THE WORLD OVER. THE ANSWER IS SURPRISINGLY SIMPLE; IT IS A DISTILLED FUNDAMENTAL ARCHETYPE.
FUNDAMENTAL ARCHETYPES ARE EASY SELLS — THE PROBLEM IS COMING UP WITH AN IDEA. YOU ALMOST HAVE TO STUMBLE UPON THEM!
SUPERMAN RETAINS THE OLDEST LINK TO THE PRISTINE FORMS. BATMAN, ON THE OTHER HAND, HAS MAINTAINED A WORTHY COMPETITIVE COUNTERPOINT TO SUPERMAN'S COMMERCIAL FOOTPRINT.
AGAIN, THE ANSWER IS SURPRIS-INGLY SIMPLE; BATMAN IS THE INVERSION TO SUPERMAN'S DISTILLED ARCHETYPE — IN THAT WAY, THE BATMAN IS ALSO A DISTILLED FUNDAMENTAL ARCHETYPE.

THE SUPERMAN ARCHETYPE TOOLBOX HAS ALL THE PARAPHERNALIA SUITABLE FOR THE MESSIANIC TYPE. HIS ALIEN HERITAGE PLACES HIM OUTSIDE PETTY NATIONALIST CONCERNS OF HUMAN TRIBES.

THE HARNESSING OF LIFE-GIVING LIGHT FOR SUPER STRENGTH, HIS IMMUTABLE HONOUR CODE, HERO OF THE DAY AND HIS UPWARD MOVEMENTS FOR FLIGHT ARE REMINISCENT OF THE STAR-BOUND PERSPECTIVE THAT HUMANS EQUATE WITH ...

BY BECOMING HUMAN, HE IS A REPACKAGED NARRATIVE FORM OF THE **HUMAN-GOD** HYBRIDS OF THE PAST.

... COMMUNING WITH THE GODS.

He comes from the world of high technology; his powers are explained by physics and his archetypal foes are manipulators or products of high technology: Lex Luthor, Brainiac, Doomsday ...

And finally, the narrative element that places Superman highest in the pantheon of gods is his fidelity to Lois Lane. Lois Lane is no second-class archetype either; she is the princess of Metropolis. Feisty, brave, possessing a bullet-proof honour code matrix, brilliant, protective of her friends and the defenseless, beautiful, articulate, mastering sophisticated social norms and yet retaining that street sass! From a biblical perspective, she is a warrior princess mirroring the only warrior princess in scripture, Deborah! The lone appearance of a warrior princess in the Bible is no cultural lapse in judgment or arbitrary play of chance. It is of significant import and we will hit it again later in our story.

Which brings us to the Batman; singularly prolific with the ladies.

His arch-villains are neither creators or creations of science, but rather, mad men and mad women; products of nature and nurture; psychopaths, sociopaths, clowns and Frankensteinian constructs. With Batman, we enter the enchanted world; the myth and mayhem of the carnival;

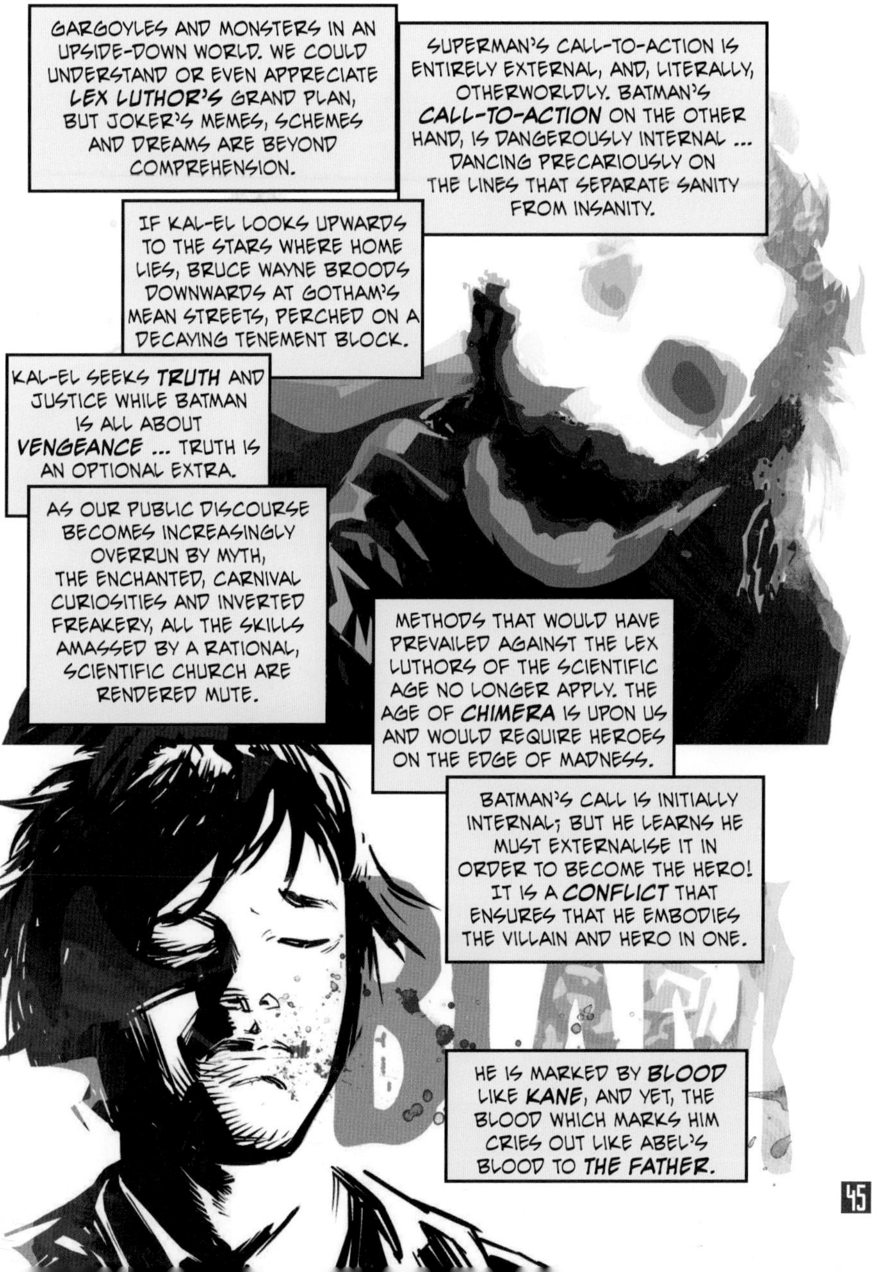
GARGOYLES AND MONSTERS IN AN UPSIDE-DOWN WORLD. WE COULD UNDERSTAND OR EVEN APPRECIATE LEX LUTHOR'S GRAND PLAN, BUT JOKER'S MEMES, SCHEMES AND DREAMS ARE BEYOND COMPREHENSION.
SUPERMAN'S CALL-TO-ACTION IS ENTIRELY EXTERNAL, AND, LITERALLY, OTHERWORLDLY. BATMAN'S CALL-TO-ACTION ON THE OTHER HAND, IS DANGEROUSLY INTERNAL ... DANCING PRECARIOUSLY ON THE LINES THAT SEPARATE SANITY FROM INSANITY.
IF KAL-EL LOOKS UPWARDS TO THE STARS WHERE HOME LIES, BRUCE WAYNE BROODS DOWNWARDS AT GOTHAM'S MEAN STREETS, PERCHED ON A DECAYING TENEMENT BLOCK.
KAL-EL SEEKS TRUTH AND JUSTICE WHILE BATMAN IS ALL ABOUT VENGEANCE ... TRUTH IS AN OPTIONAL EXTRA.
AS OUR PUBLIC DISCOURSE BECOMES INCREASINGLY OVERRUN BY MYTH, THE ENCHANTED, CARNIVAL CURIOSITIES AND INVERTED FREAKERY, ALL THE SKILLS AMASSED BY A RATIONAL, SCIENTIFIC CHURCH ARE RENDERED MUTE.
METHODS THAT WOULD HAVE PREVAILED AGAINST THE LEX LUTHORS OF THE SCIENTIFIC AGE NO LONGER APPLY. THE AGE OF CHIMERA IS UPON US AND WOULD REQUIRE HEROES ON THE EDGE OF MADNESS.
BATMAN'S CALL IS INITIALLY INTERNAL; BUT HE LEARNS HE MUST EXTERNALISE IT IN ORDER TO BECOME THE HERO! IT IS A CONFLICT THAT ENSURES THAT HE EMBODIES THE VILLAIN AND HERO IN ONE.
HE IS MARKED BY BLOOD LIKE KANE, AND YET, THE BLOOD WHICH MARKS HIM CRIES OUT LIKE ABEL'S BLOOD TO THE FATHER.

WHICH LEADS US TO THE WOMEN HE LOVES ...

THE KLEPTOMANIAC

THE ASSASSIN

THE DERANGED

IN ORDER — SELINA KYLE, TALIA AL GHUL AND POISON IVY.

BRUCE WAYNE IS STRANGELY DRAWN TO DANGEROUS WOMEN.

JUST LIKE *JESUS CHRIST* ...

THE PARALLELS WITH SUPERMAN RELATE TO UNRELATABLE ATTRIBUTES OF JESUS THE SON OF *GOD*.

THE PARALLELS WITH BATMAN RELATE TO RELATABLE ATTRIBUTES OF JESUS THE SON OF *MAN*.

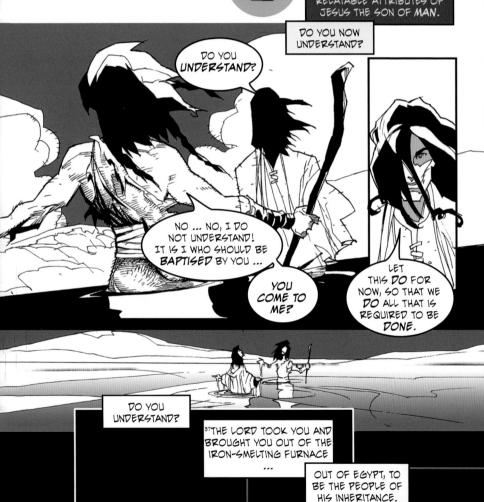

DO YOU NOW UNDERSTAND?

DO YOU *UNDERSTAND?*

NO ... NO, I DO NOT UNDERSTAND! IT IS I WHO SHOULD BE *BAPTISED* BY YOU ...

YOU COME TO ME?

LET THIS *DO* FOR NOW, SO THAT WE *DO* ALL THAT IS REQUIRED TO BE *DONE*.

DO YOU UNDERSTAND?

[37]THE LORD TOOK YOU AND BROUGHT YOU OUT OF THE IRON-SMELTING FURNACE ...

OUT OF EGYPT, TO BE THE PEOPLE OF HIS INHERITANCE.

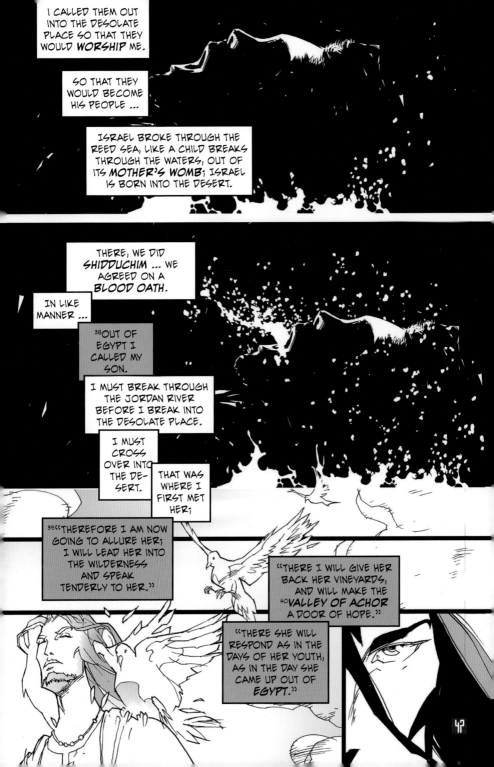

I CALLED THEM OUT INTO THE DESOLATE PLACE SO THAT THEY WOULD **WORSHIP** ME.

SO THAT THEY WOULD BECOME HIS PEOPLE ...

ISRAEL BROKE THROUGH THE REED SEA, LIKE A CHILD BREAKS THROUGH THE WATERS, OUT OF ITS **MOTHER'S WOMB**; ISRAEL IS BORN INTO THE DESERT.

THERE, WE DID **SHIDDUCHIM** ... WE AGREED ON A **BLOOD OATH.**

IN LIKE MANNER ...

38OUT OF EGYPT I CALLED MY SON.

I MUST BREAK THROUGH THE JORDAN RIVER BEFORE I BREAK INTO THE DESOLATE PLACE.

I MUST CROSS OVER INTO THE DE- SERT.

THAT WAS WHERE I FIRST MET HER;

39"THEREFORE I AM NOW GOING TO ALLURE HER; I WILL LEAD HER INTO THE WILDERNESS AND SPEAK TENDERLY TO HER."

"THERE I WILL GIVE HER BACK HER VINEYARDS, AND WILL MAKE THE 40**VALLEY OF ACHOR** A DOOR OF HOPE."

"THERE SHE WILL RESPOND AS IN THE DAYS OF HER YOUTH, AS IN THE DAY SHE CAME UP OUT OF **EGYPT.**"

REFERENCES

29. Rappers. The act of rapping is inspired by the old African practice of the *griot*. The griot holds the communal cultural memory and history of the people. Possessing formidable memory, they could single-handedly hold complete oral traditions and recite them upon request. They are known to compose praise songs for noted personalities (or even for a fee) and engage in 'battles' with another bard. We would call these *rap battles* today.

30. *"What Have You Done For Me Lately?"* Popularised by Janet Jackson in her break-out hit. Written and produced by James Harris and Terry Lewis.

31. An issue of the sexes, once voiced in the Blues, now reincarnated in Beyonce's *Single Ladies*. Written and produced by C. Tricky Stewart.

32. A popular disco era hit echoes the issues; *Ain't Nothing Going On But The Rent*. Written, performed and produced by Gwen Guthrie, Mercury Records.

33. The Message translation. A slightly truncated edit.

34. Theodore Ziolkowski in the book, *Gilgamesh Among Us: Modern Encounters With the Ancient Epic* (2011).

35. Genesis 6:2 & 4.

36. *https://www.guinnessworldrecords.com/products/books/superlatives/superhero-timeline*

37. Deuteronomy 4:20.

38. Matthew 2:15.

39. NIV translation.

40. Joshua 7:24-26.

41. Joshua 7:24-26.

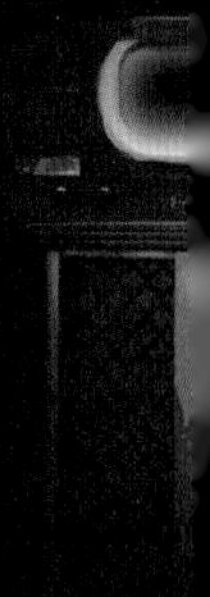

GATE THREE

TRIALS & TRIBULATIONS

GOTHAM

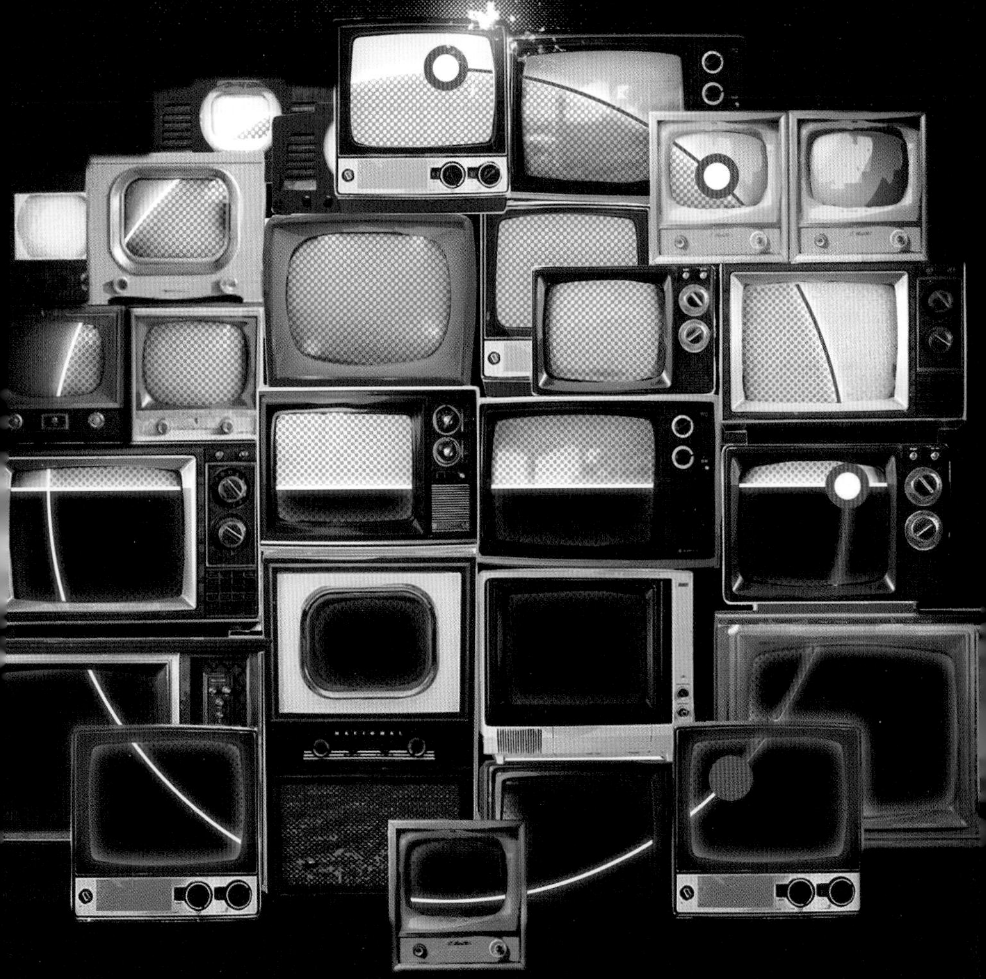

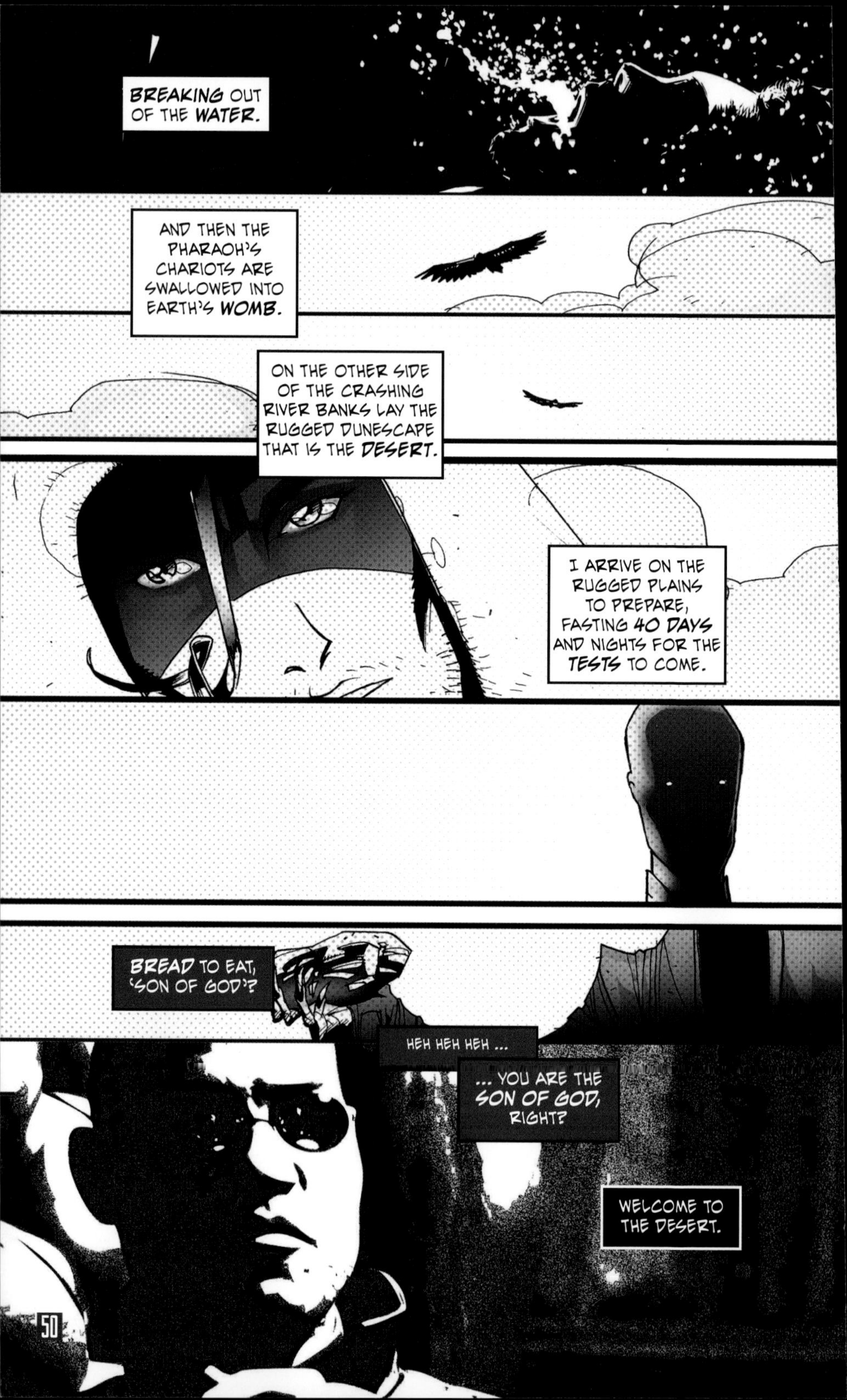
BREAKING OUT OF THE WATER.
AND THEN THE PHARAOH'S CHARIOTS ARE SWALLOWED INTO EARTH'S WOMB.
ON THE OTHER SIDE OF THE CRASHING RIVER BANKS LAY THE RUGGED DUNESCAPE THAT IS THE DESERT.
I ARRIVE ON THE RUGGED PLAINS TO PREPARE, FASTING 40 DAYS AND NIGHTS FOR THE TESTS TO COME.
BREAD TO EAT, 'SON OF GOD'?
HEH HEH HEH ...
... YOU ARE THE SON OF GOD, RIGHT?
WELCOME TO THE DESERT.

THE DESERT; WHAT IS IT?

IT'S THE ***VALLEY***. THE ***LOWEST*** PLACE ON EARTH.

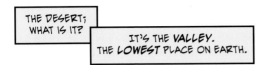

Here is how Paul would describe it:
[42]"... he had first come down from the heights of heaven, far down to the lowest parts of the earth."

David's take inspires Paul's description:
[43]"Though he leads me through the valley of the shadow of death ..."

The reader needs to read this from a topographic viewpoint; follow the text as though the writer describes the steps of the hero against terrain, then weave it into a story structure.

The hero travels down a mountain. This is implied by the presence of a deep valley; there is no valley without a mountain. Now, there are a few levels of interpretation here. There is the Moses narrative arc in play: [44]Moses ascends Mount Sinai and then descends 40 days later. Remember that when Moses returns after his 40 days in the mountains, he returns to Israel in the heat of idolatry. This is a Mosaic archetype.

But there is another level of enquiry – the mountain and valley furnishing. Imagine these two elements to be motifs or "concept bearing" patterns. Imagine they were items placed in a scene – on a conceptual stage.

The mountain is the place of God's abode and the valley is the sphere of human habitation. [45]It's something like this:

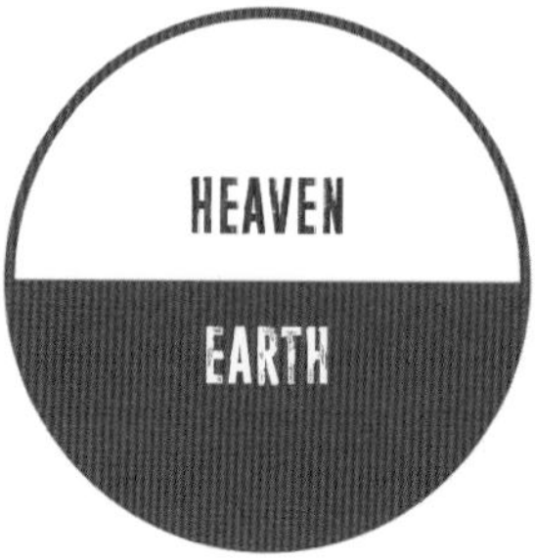
HEAVEN
EARTH

Here is our fundamental map.

The heavenly domain above is the mountain top where Moses I and Moses II (Jesus) commune with the father. The layer below is the lowest part of earth – the shadowy desolate and rugged terrain called the desert. We must push the limits of our terms in order to engage with the visceral experience David and Paul are grasping at.

Again, push the limits further; spiritual vs corporeal. Push it further still into the realm of concepts and ideas and you get [46]Proverbs 3:19's wisdom and understanding paradigm. You see how this works?

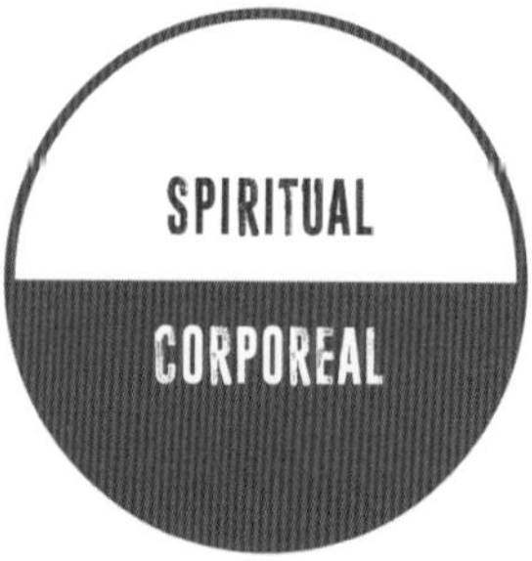
SPIRITUAL
CORPOREAL

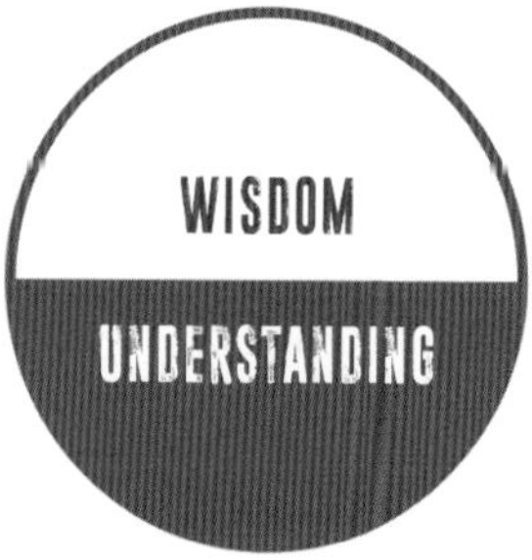
WISDOM
UNDERSTANDING

Okay. Let's pull our camera viewpoint back and narrow our focus.

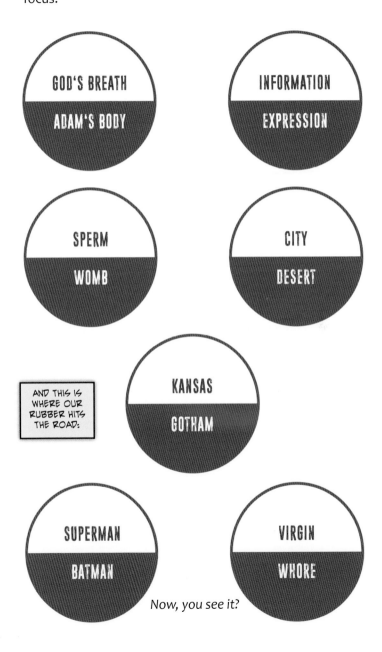

GOD'S BREATH / ADAM'S BODY

INFORMATION / EXPRESSION

SPERM / WOMB

CITY / DESERT

AND THIS IS WHERE OUR RUBBER HITS THE ROAD:

KANSAS / GOTHAM

SUPERMAN / BATMAN

VIRGIN / WHORE

Now, you see it?

The upper sphere meets the lower sphere and creates a crossing. This is a dynamic, turbulent divide. In the case of the Hebrew slaves leaving Egypt, this portal is the roaring Reed Sea which crushes the bones and skulls of the Egyptian army. It is later defined, clockwise, on the other side of 40 years as River Jordan; this is the place that crushes Israel's days of disgrace. The river, which is a dynamic portal, defines and provides language, hence Miriam's song.

CIVILISATION
RIVER JORDAN
REED SEA
DESERT

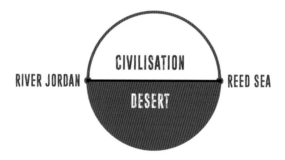

At its core is the designated sum of both realms, it gives definition to the turbulence. The sum of both realms is the archetype – that is the human of Genesis 2. This is why Adam names the animals of the garden. The human provides definition, purpose and meaning, uniting both realms. It must be read in anticipation of Adam II, Jesus Christ. Now, apply the map to the human archetype.

HEAVEN
HUMAN
EARTH

MALE
FEMALE

Let's add our hero journey layer onto our cosmic map:

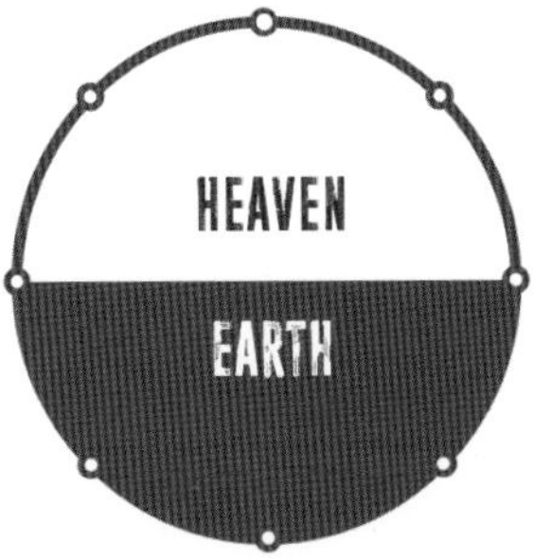
HEAVEN
EARTH

The hero marches from the highest point on the mountain top down to the depths of the desolate valley. He crosses the boundary at 3 o'clock which Jesus dramatises at his baptism, breaking into the desert for testing and proving. The desert plays as backdrop to several themes;

JESUS IN DESERT = ISRAEL'S DESERT TRAIL
JESUS IN DESERT = JESUS' INCARNATION
JESUS IN DESERT = JESUS WOOING ISRAEL ON EARTH
JESUS IN DESERT = JESUS' MINISTRY ON EARTH

Here is what Jesus' desert set piece looks like in prophecy (Hosea 3:1-4, NIV):

The Lord said to me, "Go, show your love to your wife again, though she is loved by another man and is an adulteress. Love her as the Lord loves the Israelites, though they turn to other gods and love the sacred raisin cakes."

So I bought her for fifteen shekels of silver and about a homer and a lethek of barley. Then I told her, "You are to live with me many days; you must not be a prostitute or be intimate with any man, and I will behave the same way toward you."

For the Israelites will live many days without king or prince, without sacrifice or sacred stones, without ephod or household gods.

Hosea 2:16
"In that day," declares the Lord,
"you will call me ishi (hubby);
you will no longer call me ba'ali (my master).

Beyond the rugged dunescape lay the flowing pastures of the promised land, but in this reality, the rugged dunescape extends into Jerusalem and the rest of the world. Earth is transformed into a desert; earth becomes a cosmic backdrop against which the messiah will win back his betrothed.

But this does not fit the archetype; the ultimate archetype has the virtuous warrior prince marrying the virgin warrior princess. Jesus confirms this archetype in this prayer,

John 18:9b
"I have not lost one of those You have given Me."

Clark Kent does not lose Lois Lane – Lois Lane is no whore. In a land where the hero loses the whore, we are crossing into the land of the dead and the first thing the hero does is to begin the process of dying. The gospel's narrative trajectory is Jesus' slow march downwards to death.

This land of the dead is literally the upside-down world. the world of inversions where the return of the king is sneered at. He is degraded, abused, insulted, misunderstood and, at the crucial moment in time, abandoned! In this upside-down world, nightmarish clowns resembling Heath Ledger's hunchbacked Joker run the towns and the [48]court jester is the only one capable of speaking truth.

The spiritual centre of civilisation collapses just like the days before [49]*Batman: Year One*. The synoptic gospels tell us Jesus turned out the money changers at the end of his ministry; John tells us he did it at the beginning of his ministry. Just as in *Batman: Year One*, the first act is the cleansing of the Temple, the second act is the judgment of the Temple.

The template of villainy is given to us in 1 Samuel 8:11-18. Absalom the Usurper is about to fulfil his internally-generated call as an archetype. He crosses over to the land of the dead, but not to die ... he crosses over to 'live'! Jesus is driven into Gotham so he might die. At the core of this narrative structure is a certain 'Batman-esque dysfunctionality' – Jesus is in the land of the dead in pursuit of Selina Kyle, a lover who is just as likely to stick a knife in his back as she is to kiss him smack-bang on the lips.

John is now dead and Jesus' love of a dangerous woman is about to kill him.

REFERENCES

42. Ephesians 4:9. The Living Bible. Paul is exegeting Psalm 68:18.

43. Psalm 23:4.

44. Exodus 32.

45. For a thorough investigation into the ancient pre-platonic biblical view of cosmic symbolism, see Matthew Pageau's *The Language of Creation*. The biblical cosmic map is antithetical to the platonic cosmic map. Unfortunately, the platonic map's footprint accounts for a great deal in Western theology. Refer to Francis Schaeffer's work (*Escape From Reason*, Chapter One) for comparison's to Matthew Pageau's paradigm.

46. Also: Proverbs 4:7, 24:3, Jeremiah 51:15.

47. Alas, page limits restrict what can be said in this volume, however, this much can be said in the footnote section – the dividing line is the dynamic third element of the two compartments. In Proverbs it is called 'knowledge'; from a geological perspective, it is the river. You would remember that various black spirituals reference *the river* as the portal between one world into the other. We may define this stasis as a category of truth, reality, metaphysical language ... I have defined it here as the archetype.

48. Shakepheare's *King Lear's* Jester. In the gospels, the role is played by John the Baptiser.

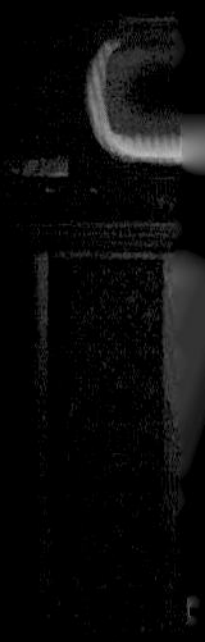

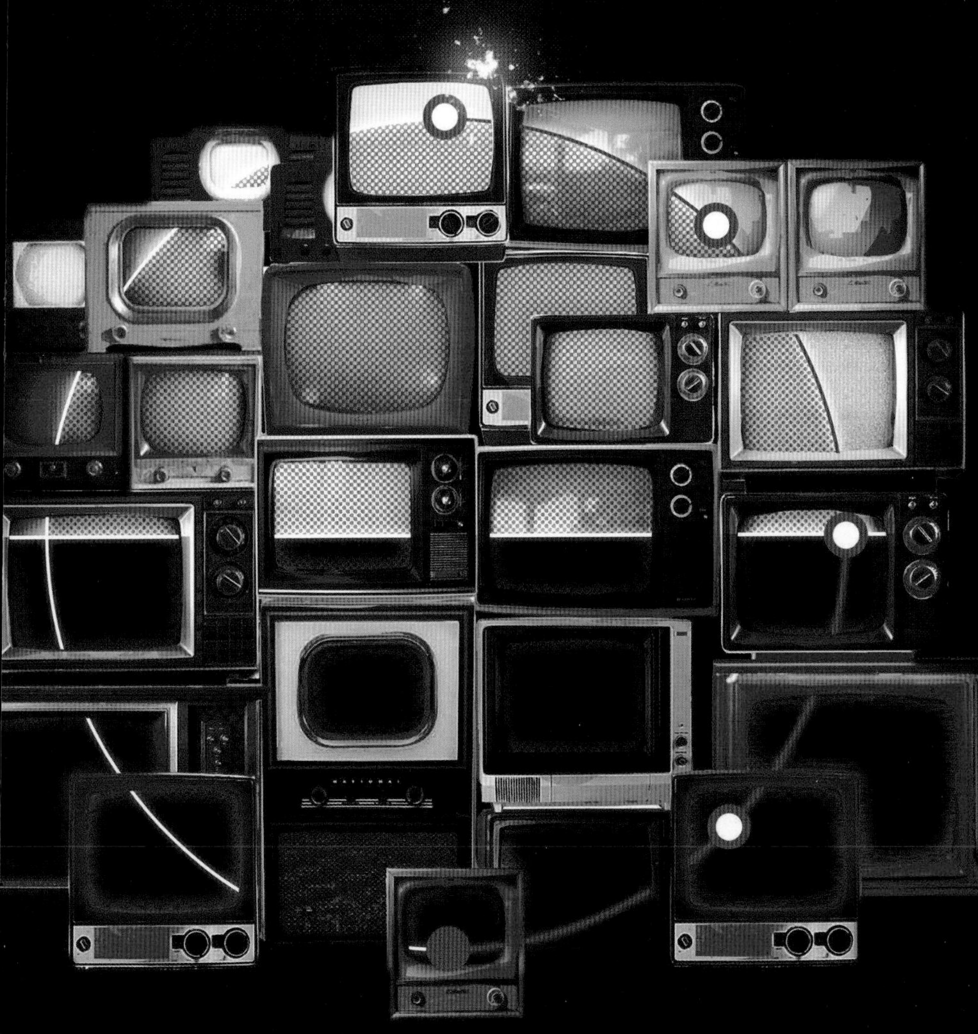
NATIONAL

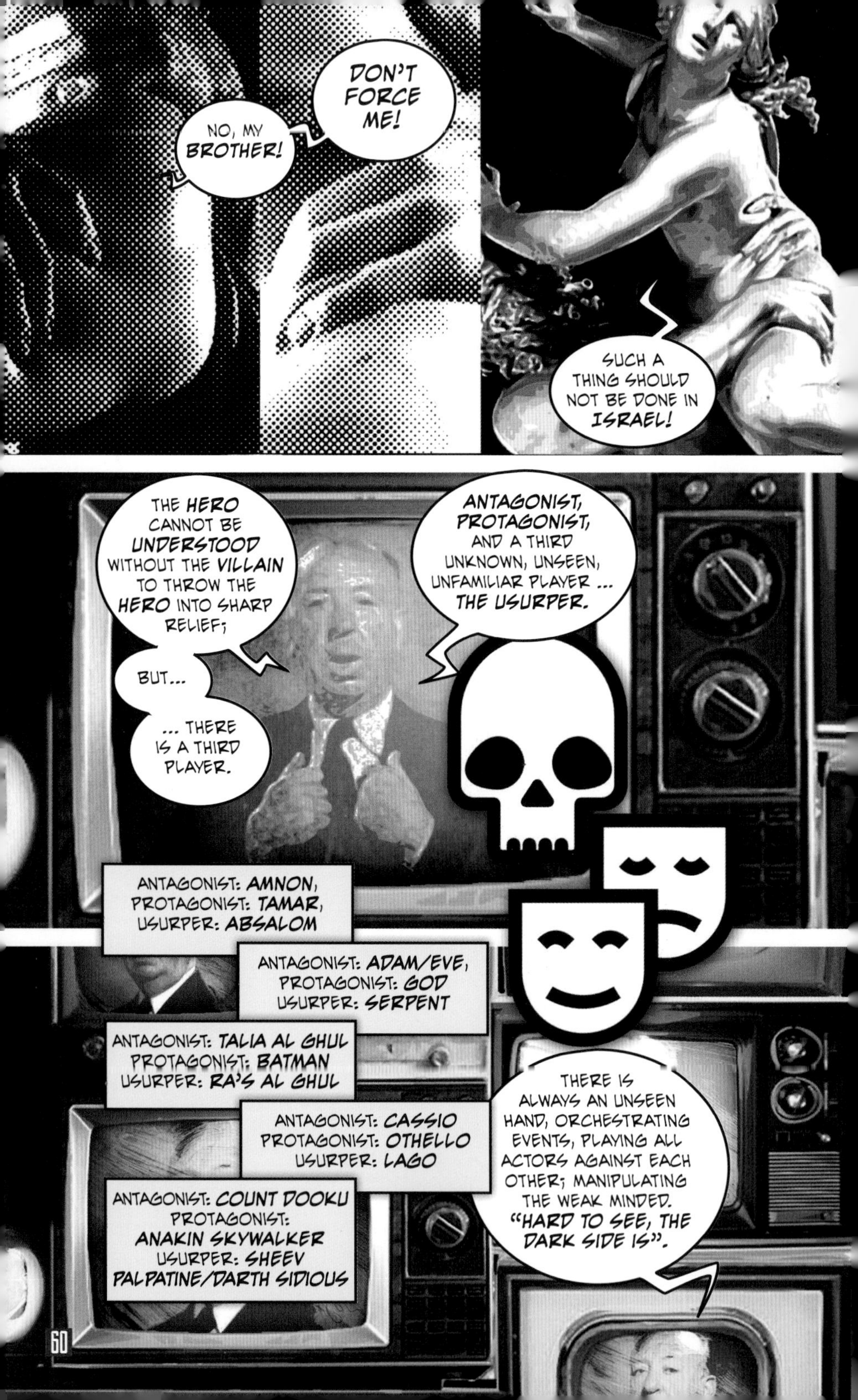
NO, MY BROTHER!
DON'T FORCE ME!
SUCH A THING SHOULD NOT BE DONE IN ISRAEL!
THE HERO CANNOT BE UNDERSTOOD WITHOUT THE VILLAIN TO THROW THE HERO INTO SHARP RELIEF;
BUT...
... THERE IS A THIRD PLAYER.
ANTAGONIST, PROTAGONIST, AND A THIRD UNKNOWN, UNSEEN, UNFAMILIAR PLAYER ... THE USURPER.
ANTAGONIST: AMNON, PROTAGONIST: TAMAR, USURPER: ABSALOM
ANTAGONIST: ADAM/EVE, PROTAGONIST: GOD USURPER: SERPENT
ANTAGONIST: TALIA AL GHUL PROTAGONIST: BATMAN USURPER: RA'S AL GHUL
ANTAGONIST: CASSIO PROTAGONIST: OTHELLO USURPER: LAGO
ANTAGONIST: COUNT DOOKU PROTAGONIST: ANAKIN SKYWALKER USURPER: SHEEV PALPATINE/DARTH SIDIOUS
THERE IS ALWAYS AN UNSEEN HAND, ORCHESTRATING EVENTS, PLAYING ALL ACTORS AGAINST EACH OTHER; MANIPULATING THE WEAK MINDED. "HARD TO SEE, THE DARK SIDE IS".

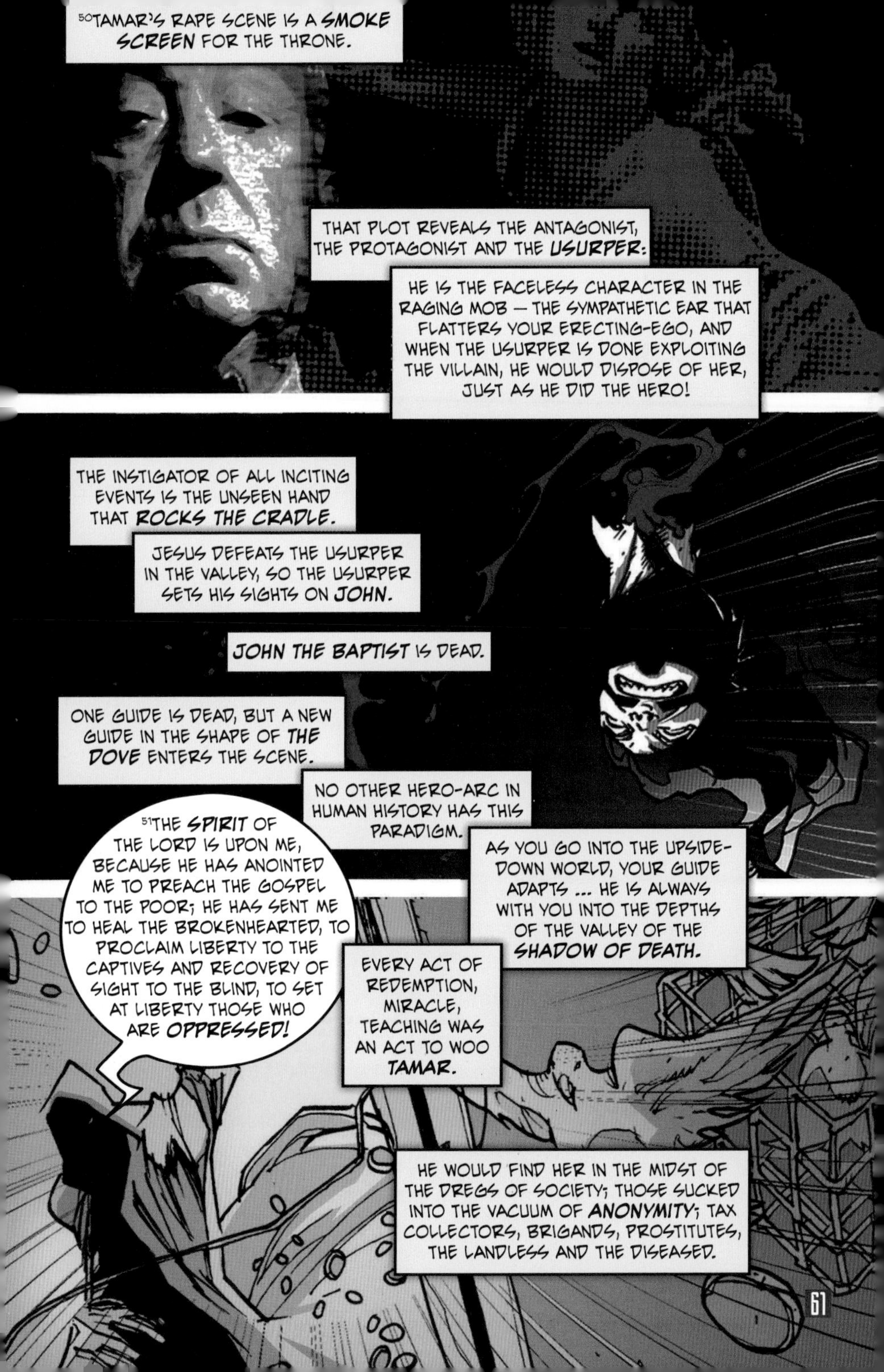

[50]TAMAR'S RAPE SCENE IS A SMOKE SCREEN FOR THE THRONE.
THAT PLOT REVEALS THE ANTAGONIST, THE PROTAGONIST AND THE USURPER:
HE IS THE FACELESS CHARACTER IN THE RAGING MOB — THE SYMPATHETIC EAR THAT FLATTERS YOUR ERECTING-EGO, AND WHEN THE USURPER IS DONE EXPLOITING THE VILLAIN, HE WOULD DISPOSE OF HER, JUST AS HE DID THE HERO!
THE INSTIGATOR OF ALL INCITING EVENTS IS THE UNSEEN HAND THAT ROCKS THE CRADLE.
JESUS DEFEATS THE USURPER IN THE VALLEY, SO THE USURPER SETS HIS SIGHTS ON JOHN.
JOHN THE BAPTIST IS DEAD.
ONE GUIDE IS DEAD, BUT A NEW GUIDE IN THE SHAPE OF THE DOVE ENTERS THE SCENE.
NO OTHER HERO-ARC IN HUMAN HISTORY HAS THIS PARADIGM.
[51]THE SPIRIT OF THE LORD IS UPON ME, BECAUSE HE HAS ANOINTED ME TO PREACH THE GOSPEL TO THE POOR; HE HAS SENT ME TO HEAL THE BROKENHEARTED, TO PROCLAIM LIBERTY TO THE CAPTIVES AND RECOVERY OF SIGHT TO THE BLIND, TO SET AT LIBERTY THOSE WHO ARE OPPRESSED!
AS YOU GO INTO THE UPSIDE-DOWN WORLD, YOUR GUIDE ADAPTS ... HE IS ALWAYS WITH YOU INTO THE DEPTHS OF THE VALLEY OF THE SHADOW OF DEATH.
EVERY ACT OF REDEMPTION, MIRACLE, TEACHING WAS AN ACT TO WOO TAMAR.
HE WOULD FIND HER IN THE MIDST OF THE DREGS OF SOCIETY; THOSE SUCKED INTO THE VACUUM OF ANONYMITY; TAX COLLECTORS, BRIGANDS, PROSTITUTES, THE LANDLESS AND THE DISEASED.

The narrative trajectory of the gospels hurls toward Golgotha. Jesus is always heading *up* toward Jerusalem as he journeys southward from his base in Galilee toward his destiny, Jerusalem. Regardless of his starting point, he is always heading *upwards* toward Jerusalem!

Matthew 20:18
We are going up to Jerusalem,
and the Son of Man will be delivered over to the
chief priests and the teachers of the law.

LUKE 2:22
MARK 10:32
MARK 15:41
MARK 10:33
LUKE 2:42
JOHN 2:13
JOHN 5:1

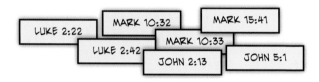

His story darkens like a rain-soaked, Nolan-directed, *Dark Knight* treatment. The atmosphere progressively thickens and begins to press upon the messiah, weighing heavy upon his psyche. The disciples, starting to taste the dread approaching, now anticipate a misadventure from what once seemed like an adventure of a lifetime! As the sky darkens, they press on; *up* towards Jerusalem. One disciple would peel off. The *woman with the alabaster jar* event was one more baffling event too far.

JERUSALEM, JERUSALEM, YOU WHO KILL THE PROPHETS AND STONE THOSE SENT TO YOU, HOW OFTEN I HAVE LONGED TO GATHER YOUR CHILDREN TOGETHER, AS A HEN GATHERS HER CHICKS UNDER HER WINGS, AND YOU WERE NOT WILLING!

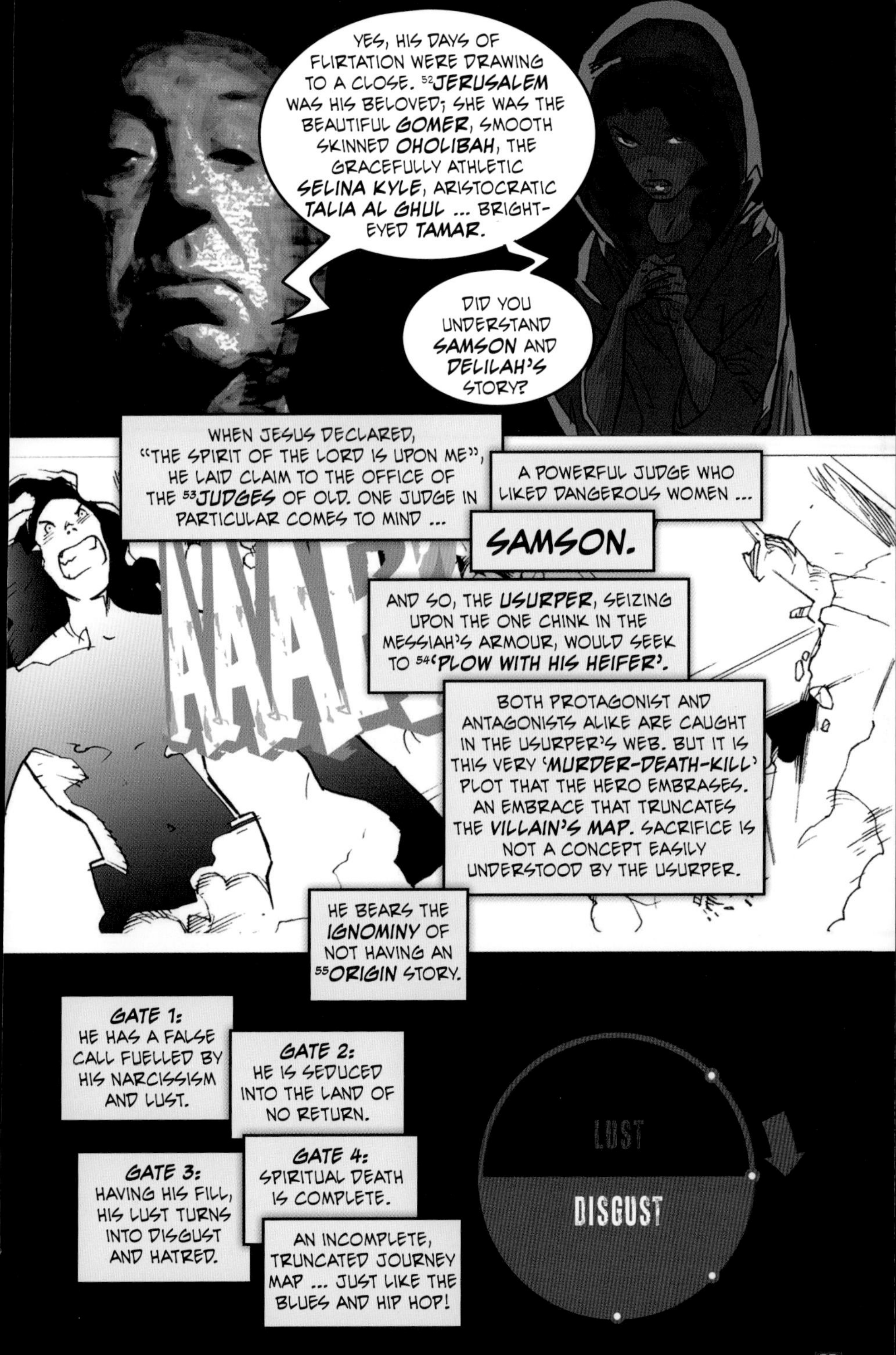
YES, HIS DAYS OF FLIRTATION WERE DRAWING TO A CLOSE. [52]JERUSALEM WAS HIS BELOVED; SHE WAS THE BEAUTIFUL GOMER, SMOOTH SKINNED OHOLIBAH, THE GRACEFULLY ATHLETIC SELINA KYLE, ARISTOCRATIC TALIA AL GHUL ... BRIGHT-EYED TAMAR.
DID YOU UNDERSTAND SAMSON AND DELILAH'S STORY?
WHEN JESUS DECLARED, "THE SPIRIT OF THE LORD IS UPON ME", HE LAID CLAIM TO THE OFFICE OF THE [53]JUDGES OF OLD. ONE JUDGE IN PARTICULAR COMES TO MIND ...
A POWERFUL JUDGE WHO LIKED DANGEROUS WOMEN ...
SAMSON.
AND SO, THE USURPER, SEIZING UPON THE ONE CHINK IN THE MESSIAH'S ARMOUR, WOULD SEEK TO [54]'PLOW WITH HIS HEIFER'.
BOTH PROTAGONIST AND ANTAGONISTS ALIKE ARE CAUGHT IN THE USURPER'S WEB. BUT IT IS THIS VERY 'MURDER-DEATH-KILL' PLOT THAT THE HERO EMBRASES. AN EMBRACE THAT TRUNCATES THE VILLAIN'S MAP. SACRIFICE IS NOT A CONCEPT EASILY UNDERSTOOD BY THE USURPER.
HE BEARS THE IGNOMINY OF NOT HAVING AN [55]ORIGIN STORY.
GATE 1: HE HAS A FALSE CALL FUELLED BY HIS NARCISSISM AND LUST.
GATE 2: HE IS SEDUCED INTO THE LAND OF NO RETURN.
GATE 3: HAVING HIS FILL, HIS LUST TURNS INTO DISGUST AND HATRED.
GATE 4: SPIRITUAL DEATH IS COMPLETE.
AN INCOMPLETE, TRUNCATED JOURNEY MAP ... JUST LIKE THE BLUES AND HIP HOP!
LUST
DISGUST

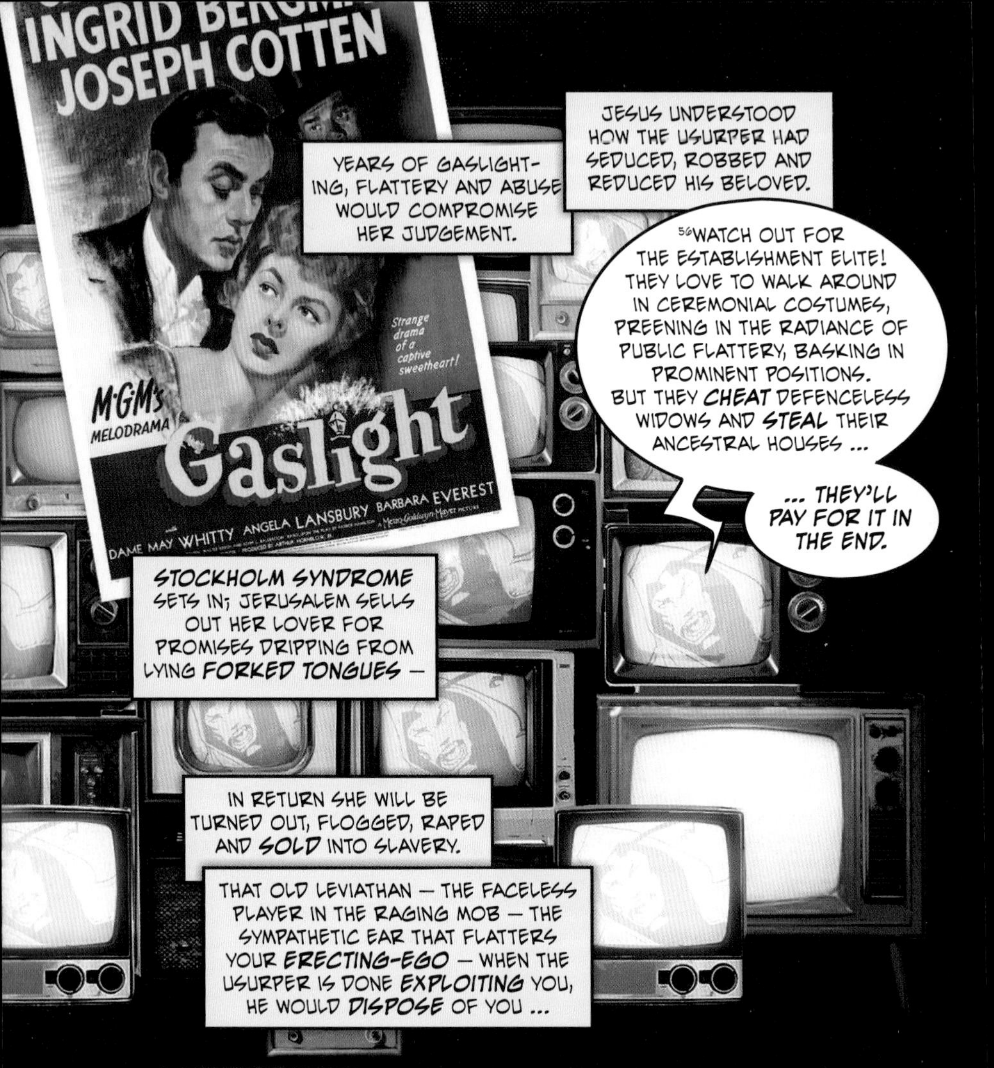
JOSEPH COTTEN
Strange drama of a captive sweetheart!
M·G·M's MELODRAMA
Gaslight
DAME MAY WHITTY ANGELA LANSBURY BARBARA EVEREST
YEARS OF GASLIGHTING, FLATTERY AND ABUSE WOULD COMPROMISE HER JUDGEMENT.
JESUS UNDERSTOOD HOW THE USURPER HAD SEDUCED, ROBBED AND REDUCED HIS BELOVED.
[56]WATCH OUT FOR THE ESTABLISHMENT ELITE! THEY LOVE TO WALK AROUND IN CEREMONIAL COSTUMES, PREENING IN THE RADIANCE OF PUBLIC FLATTERY, BASKING IN PROMINENT POSITIONS. BUT THEY **CHEAT** DEFENCELESS WIDOWS AND **STEAL** THEIR ANCESTRAL HOUSES ...
... THEY'LL PAY FOR IT IN THE END.
STOCKHOLM SYNDROME SETS IN; JERUSALEM SELLS OUT HER LOVER FOR PROMISES DRIPPING FROM LYING **FORKED TONGUES** –
IN RETURN SHE WILL BE TURNED OUT, FLOGGED, RAPED AND **SOLD** INTO SLAVERY.
THAT OLD LEVIATHAN – THE FACELESS PLAYER IN THE RAGING MOB – THE SYMPATHETIC EAR THAT FLATTERS YOUR **ERECTING-EGO** – WHEN THE USURPER IS DONE **EXPLOITING** YOU, HE WOULD **DISPOSE** OF YOU ...

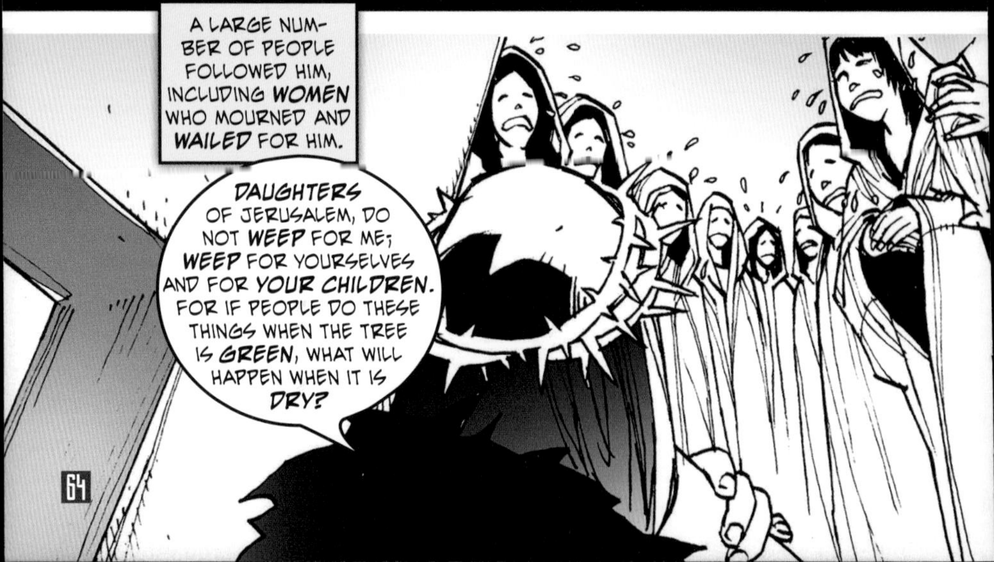
A LARGE NUMBER OF PEOPLE FOLLOWED HIM, INCLUDING **WOMEN** WHO MOURNED AND **WAILED** FOR HIM.
DAUGHTERS OF JERUSALEM, DO NOT **WEEP** FOR ME; **WEEP** FOR YOURSELVES AND FOR **YOUR CHILDREN.** FOR IF PEOPLE DO THESE THINGS WHEN THE TREE IS **GREEN**, WHAT WILL HAPPEN WHEN IT IS **DRY?**

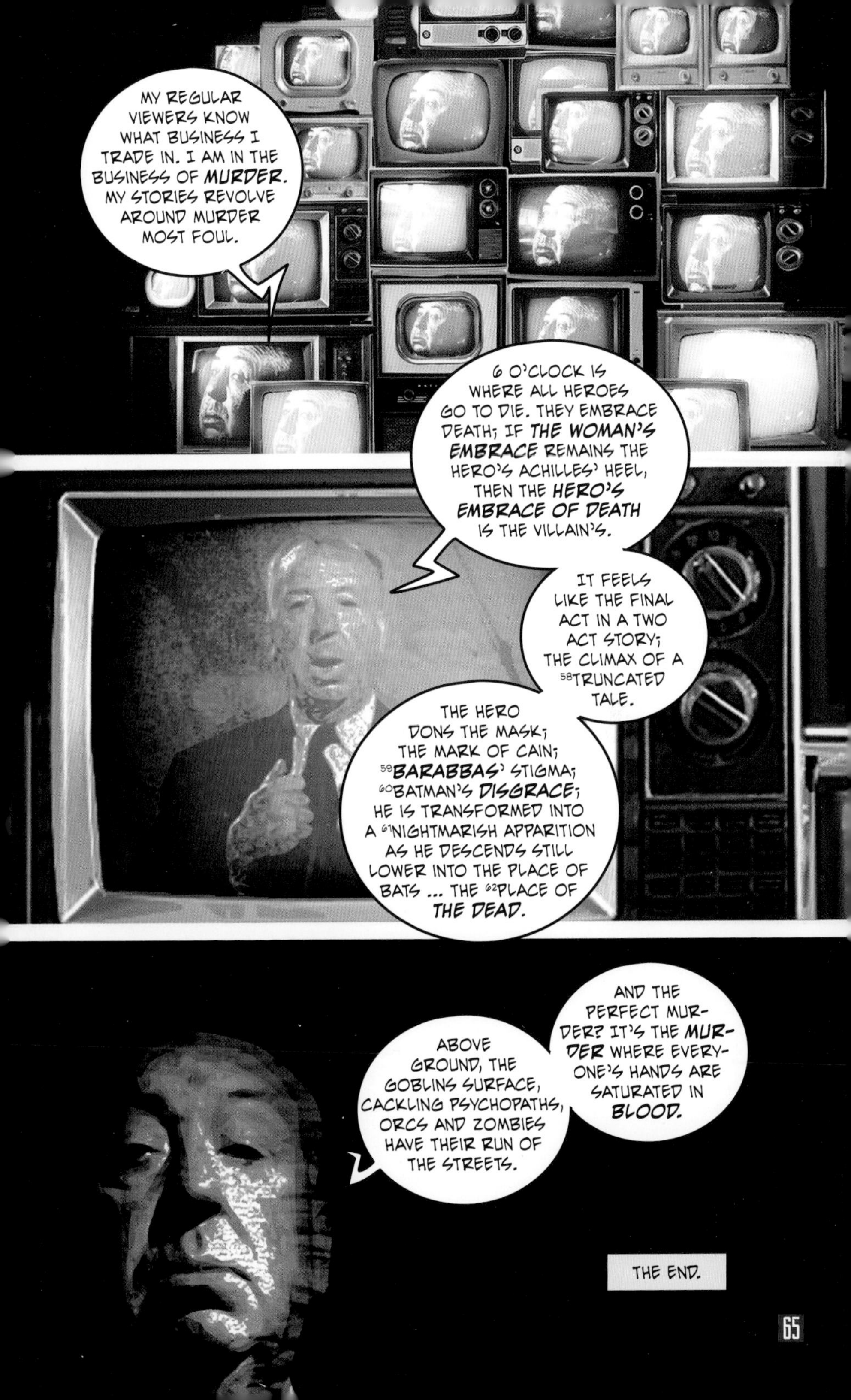
MY REGULAR VIEWERS KNOW WHAT BUSINESS I TRADE IN. I AM IN THE BUSINESS OF **MURDER.** MY STORIES REVOLVE AROUND MURDER MOST FOUL.
6 O'CLOCK IS WHERE ALL HEROES GO TO DIE. THEY EMBRACE DEATH; IF **THE WOMAN'S EMBRACE** REMAINS THE HERO'S ACHILLES' HEEL, THEN THE **HERO'S EMBRACE OF DEATH** IS THE VILLAIN'S.
IT FEELS LIKE THE FINAL ACT IN A TWO ACT STORY; THE CLIMAX OF A [58]TRUNCATED TALE.
THE HERO DONS THE MASK; THE MARK OF CAIN; [59]**BARABBAS'** STIGMA; [60]BATMAN'S **DISGRACE**; HE IS TRANSFORMED INTO A [61]NIGHTMARISH APPARITION AS HE DESCENDS STILL LOWER INTO THE PLACE OF BATS ... THE [62]PLACE OF **THE DEAD.**
ABOVE GROUND, THE GOBLINS SURFACE, CACKLING PSYCHOPATHS, ORCS AND ZOMBIES HAVE THEIR RUN OF THE STREETS.
AND THE PERFECT MURDER? IT'S THE **MURDER** WHERE EVERYONE'S HANDS ARE SATURATED IN **BLOOD.**
THE END.

REFERENCES

49. *Batman: Year One* by Frank Miller.

50. 2 Samuel 13. For a detailed investigation, see Phyllis Trible. *Texts of Terror*. Chapter 2: Tamar: the Royal Rape of Wisdom.

51. Luke 4:18 NKJV. Judges 3:10.

52. Isaiah 62:1-11.

53. Judges 3:10. The Spirit of the Lord came upon him, and he judged Israel. He went out to war, and the Lord delivered Cushan-Rishathaim king of Mesopotamia into his hand; and his hand prevailed over Cushan-Rishathaim. (This is the oldest expression of the form in scripture.)

54. Judges 14:18.

55. Satan has no origin story. All accounts of an origin story are adventurous ... at best. Such assumptions do not appreciate the disgrace of having one's name stripped in the old world.

56. Mark 12:38-39 (my amplification and partial translation from The Message).

57. Luke 23:27, 28, 31 New International Version. Hosea 10:8.

58. Truncated tale: as in, a story or song cut short of its natural resolved length.

59. Matthew 27.

60. *The Dark Knight*. In Spite of being Gotham's saviour, Batman ends up public enemy No 1. This is a repeating motif in all Batman universes.

61. Isaiah 52:14.

62. The historically evolving Hebrew motif, *sheol*, is used here. This is not equivalent to the Greek paradigm, *hades*. The Hebrew sense counterpoints between, nothingness, poetic justice, God's holiness, physical burial place, irony and promise of resurrection of the righteous.

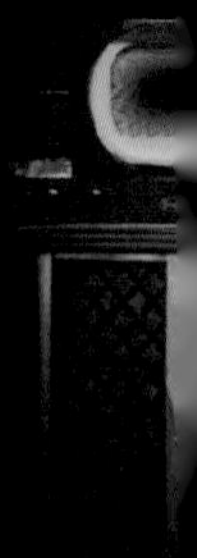

THE MORPH

BOY MEETS GIRL ... AGAIN

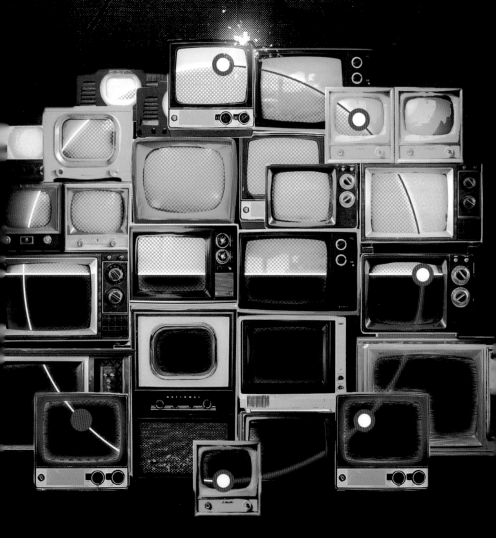

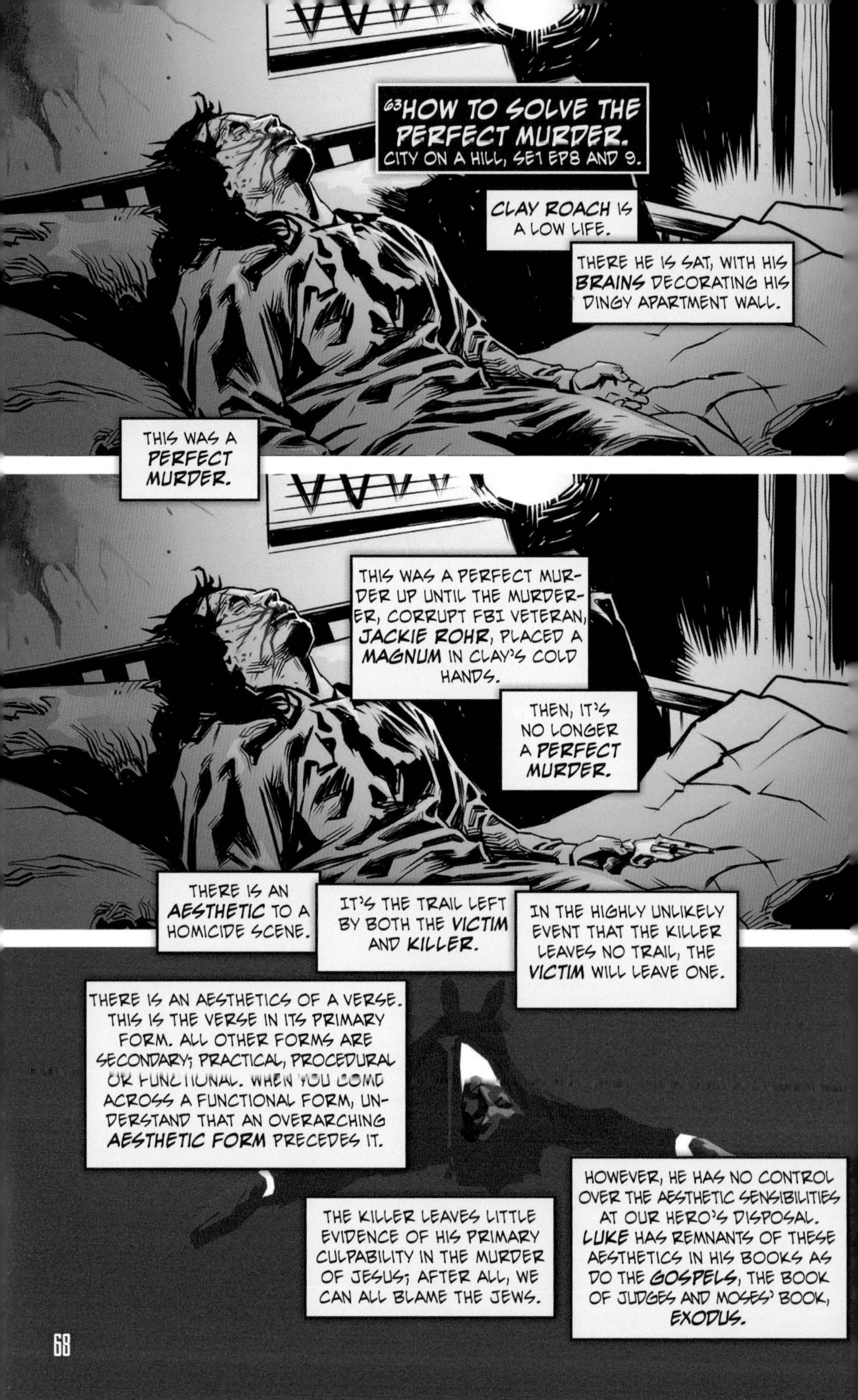

63 HOW TO SOLVE THE PERFECT MURDER. CITY ON A HILL, SE1 EP8 AND 9.
CLAY ROACH IS A LOW LIFE.
THERE HE IS SAT, WITH HIS BRAINS DECORATING HIS DINGY APARTMENT WALL.
THIS WAS A PERFECT MURDER.
THIS WAS A PERFECT MURDER UP UNTIL THE MURDERER, CORRUPT FBI VETERAN, JACKIE ROHR, PLACED A MAGNUM IN CLAY'S COLD HANDS.
THEN, IT'S NO LONGER A PERFECT MURDER.
THERE IS AN AESTHETIC TO A HOMICIDE SCENE.
IT'S THE TRAIL LEFT BY BOTH THE VICTIM AND KILLER.
IN THE HIGHLY UNLIKELY EVENT THAT THE KILLER LEAVES NO TRAIL, THE VICTIM WILL LEAVE ONE.
THERE IS AN AESTHETICS OF A VERSE. THIS IS THE VERSE IN ITS PRIMARY FORM. ALL OTHER FORMS ARE SECONDARY; PRACTICAL, PROCEDURAL OR FUNCTIONAL. WHEN YOU COME ACROSS A FUNCTIONAL FORM, UNDERSTAND THAT AN OVERARCHING AESTHETIC FORM PRECEDES IT.
THE KILLER LEAVES LITTLE EVIDENCE OF HIS PRIMARY CULPABILITY IN THE MURDER OF JESUS; AFTER ALL, WE CAN ALL BLAME THE JEWS.
HOWEVER, HE HAS NO CONTROL OVER THE AESTHETIC SENSIBILITIES AT OUR HERO'S DISPOSAL. LUKE HAS REMNANTS OF THESE AESTHETICS IN HIS BOOKS AS DO THE GOSPELS, THE BOOK OF JUDGES AND MOSES' BOOK, EXODUS.

It's not so much setting up a perfect murder as setting up a perfect trap. You see, Jesus had been setting up the murder scene from way back in the days of patriachs. We reach a defining narrative peak as the Hebrew slave nation on the run attempts a miraculous crossing of the Sea of Reeds. The book of Exodus sets up the instigating actors of the story; every actor anticipates and drives each new story section. They also anticipate the birth of a new nation.

SHIPHRAH AND PUAH: MIDWIVES.

JOCHEBED AND MIRIAM: MOTHER AND BABY PROTECTOR.

PHARAOH'S DAUGHTER: ADOPTIVE MOTHER.

ZIPPORA: 'WOMAN AT THE WELL' ARCHETYPE.

FEMALE CHORISTERS: PROVIDING LANGUAGE TO [64]PREVERBAL NATION.

[65]**GOD THE MIDWIFE.**

Even inanimate objects get cast as women:

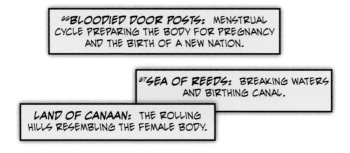

[66]**BLOODIED DOOR POSTS:** MENSTRUAL CYCLE PREPARING THE BODY FOR PREGNANCY AND THE BIRTH OF A NEW NATION.

[67]**SEA OF REEDS:** BREAKING WATERS AND BIRTHING CANAL.

LAND OF CANAAN: THE ROLLING HILLS RESEMBLING THE FEMALE BODY.

[68]Milk and honey as produced by mother's breasts.

Luke methodically replicates this aesthetic by populating origin-story components with 'women'.

> *Luke 1: the birth of the guide and the hero.*
> *Luke 8:2-4: women finance the hero's mission.*
> *Luke 23:27: distinct category –*
> *women mourn his walk of shame.*
> *Luke 23:45: distinct category –*
> *women remain faithful to the hero in his final hours.*
> *Luke 23:55, 24: 1: women remain faithful*
> *beyond the hero's death.*
> *Luke 24:10, 22, 24: women were first witnesses*
> *of the new age.*

[69]Luke would speak more about women than all the other gospels combined. In addition to his book of *Acts*, he would mention women more than the rest of the books of the New Testament ... combined!

Narcissists are compromised by a debilitating lack of self-awareness. This provides predictable blindspots and it is in this field of view that Jesus sets up the next scene. The proliferation of women in Bible plot points is an indication of an origin story. But we already know Jesus's origin story, so whose origin story is in view here?

Luke, as Moses did *back in the day*, is hinting at an origin story. An origin story crafted – as in the days of Moses – in the red-hot cauldron of the upside-down world right inside Satan's backyard ... the very last place to look for a hero and the very wrong type of hero.

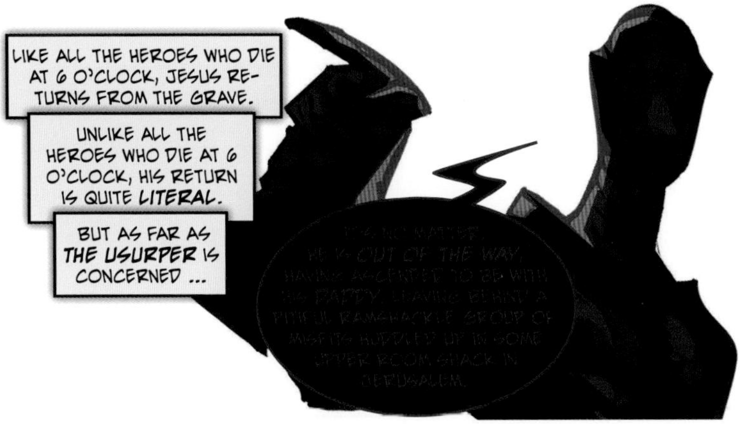
LIKE ALL THE HEROES WHO DIE AT 6 O'CLOCK, JESUS RE-TURNS FROM THE GRAVE.
UNLIKE ALL THE HEROES WHO DIE AT 6 O'CLOCK, HIS RETURN IS QUITE LITERAL.
BUT AS FAR AS THE USURPER IS CONCERNED ...
IT'S NO MATTER. HE IS OUT OF THE WAY, HAVING ASCENDED TO BE WITH HIS DADDY, LEAVING BEHIND A PITIFUL RAMSHACKLE GROUP OF MISFITS HUDDLED UP IN SOME UPPER ROOM SHACK IN JERUSALEM.

What little vision ...

It was a bait and switch operation. The strongest clue about Jesus' real mission is given in John 18:9.

OF THOSE WHOM YOU GAVE ME I HAVE LOST NONE.

There's another strong clue in the ancient account from the book of Judges. Israel's second generation finally crosses the Jordan river at 9 o'clock. The first generation, having perished, just like Hip Hop, at 6 o'clock, is resuscitated in the guise of second generation. The second generation, under the leadership of General Joshua, would cross the Jordan and destroy Jericho. At the end of their campaign, they would destroy 31 of 62 kingdoms in Canaan.

It would take another 200 years for the other 31 kingdoms to be vanquished. That campaign would be overseen by General Deborah – the warrior prophetess. Deborah completes the work of Joshua (meaning, Saviour).

[70]DC's 2017 superhero movie *Wonder Woman* is surprisingly instructive. At the closing stage of the final act, Wonder Woman's destiny is about to be altered. Her lover, Steve Taylor, hijacks a bomber loaded with a weapon of mass destruction toxin, taking it up to safe distance at high altitude where he detonates the bomber, destroying the toxin. Steve Taylor's ultimate sacrifice unleashes Wonder Woman's latent powers.

Seeing her lover, Steve, offer himself up for the world resolves her cognitive dissonance, releasing her full potential.

This was the plan all along; the hero offers himself as bait, then switches the play; the cognitive dissonance at 1 o'clock (Gate 1: The Call) is resolved at 6 o'clock (Gate 4: The Abyss). Jesus plays out the dissonance in this rhetorical refrain:

[71]**MY-GOD, MY GOD,** WHY HAVE YOU **FORSAKEN** ME?

HIS CONFLICT AND RESOLVE IS REAL; BUT THERE IS ANOTHER COGNITIVE PARALYSIS IN PLAY;

THAT PARALYSIS TO BE FOUND IN *HIS WOMAN* AND IT IS HERE THAT WE DISCOVER THE DEVIL'S *BLIND SPOT.*

EVERYBODY DIES AT 6 O'CLOCK. LIKE HIP HOP AND THE BLUES, THE OL' TURNTABLE STYLUS KEEPS SKIPPING, BUMPING AND GRINDING THE OLD REFRAIN AT 6 O'CLOCK:
"%^$ YOU... BITCH!
"%^$ YOU... BITCH!
"%^$ YOU... BITCH!
THAT IS WHAT GENERATIONAL ABUSE DOES TO THE PSYCHE. YOU KEEP BUMPING AND GRINDING TO THE SAME OLD STUTTER;
STOCKHOLM SYNDROME KEEPING YOUR GAZE FIXED ON THE ***PHALLIC ERECTION*** WHICH IS YOUR OWN EGO; A NAVEL-GAZING EXERCISE IF THERE EVER WAS ONE.

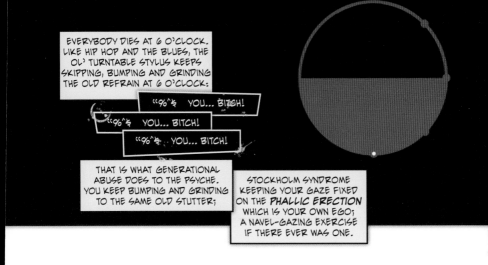

The hero gives his life freely... breaking the transfixed gaze by his resurrection from the grave.

[72]In spite of her betrayal, his faithful love to her restores her sanity! The devil-woman who hedges her bets – here today, stabbing ya tomorrow – fair-weather lover, emotionally crippled by hundreds of years of gaslighting, is broken free of the hypnotic gaze.

The hero's resuscitation in popular culture's narrative arc is a transformed character. In this hero arc, however, Jesus' resurrection [73]drags his betrothed with him from the grave! His resurrection is her metamorphosis! Here is the satan's fatal and progressively debilitating blind spot!

After his ascension, she would await the [74]*mattan* at [75]Solomon's Colonnade on the Eastern wall of the Temple courts in Jerusalem and the [76]*mattan* he leaves behind would be a game-changing ticking bomb.

REFERENCES

63. How to solve a murder: *The Wire* SE1 EP4 at 5minutes. McNulty and Bunk in honour of the real life detective, Terry McLarney, who is quoted in the novel (which inspired *The Wire* TV series), *Homicide: A Year of the Killing Streets* by David Simon. This legendary, visceral four-letter-word ridden scene mirrors one of my reading methods.

64. Exodus 14:11-12.

65. Ezekiel 16:4-8. Postnatal care was an all-woman affair in the ancient world. First breath Ex 15:8, 18.

66. Exodus 12:13.

67. *Culture of the Jews*. Volume One. Ed; David Biale. Chapter One; *Imagining the Birth of Ancient Israel: National Metaphors in the Bible*. Ilana Pardes. 2002 Schocken Books, New York. Also; Opener of the womb: Exodus 13:2. Matthew 2:13-15.

68. Songs 4:11.

69. Acts 1:14, 5:14, 8:3, 8:12, 9:2, 13:50, 16:13, 17:4, 12, 22:4.

70. *Wonder Woman*, 2017 movie. Warner Bros. Pictures. Directed by Patty Jenkins.

71. Mark 15:34, Psalm 22:1.

72. Hosea 3:1. "Go show love to your wife again!"

73. Colossians 2:12.

74. Mohar is a marriage dowry paid by the father of the groom to the father of the bride. Mattan is a voluntary gift given to the bride by the groom. Upon acceptance of mohar, the couple are formally wedded. After the mohar is paid, there is a gap year for logistical preparation before ceremonial marriage. The mattan (gift) symbolises the torah in Old Testament spirituality.

75. Luke 24:53.

76. Mattan represents the Holy Spirit in New testament spirituality. Ephesians 4:8 – The gift of the Holy Spirit. Acts 1:4-5, 2:1-13, Romans 12:6.

GATE SIX

THE CROSSING II

LEAVING GOTHAM

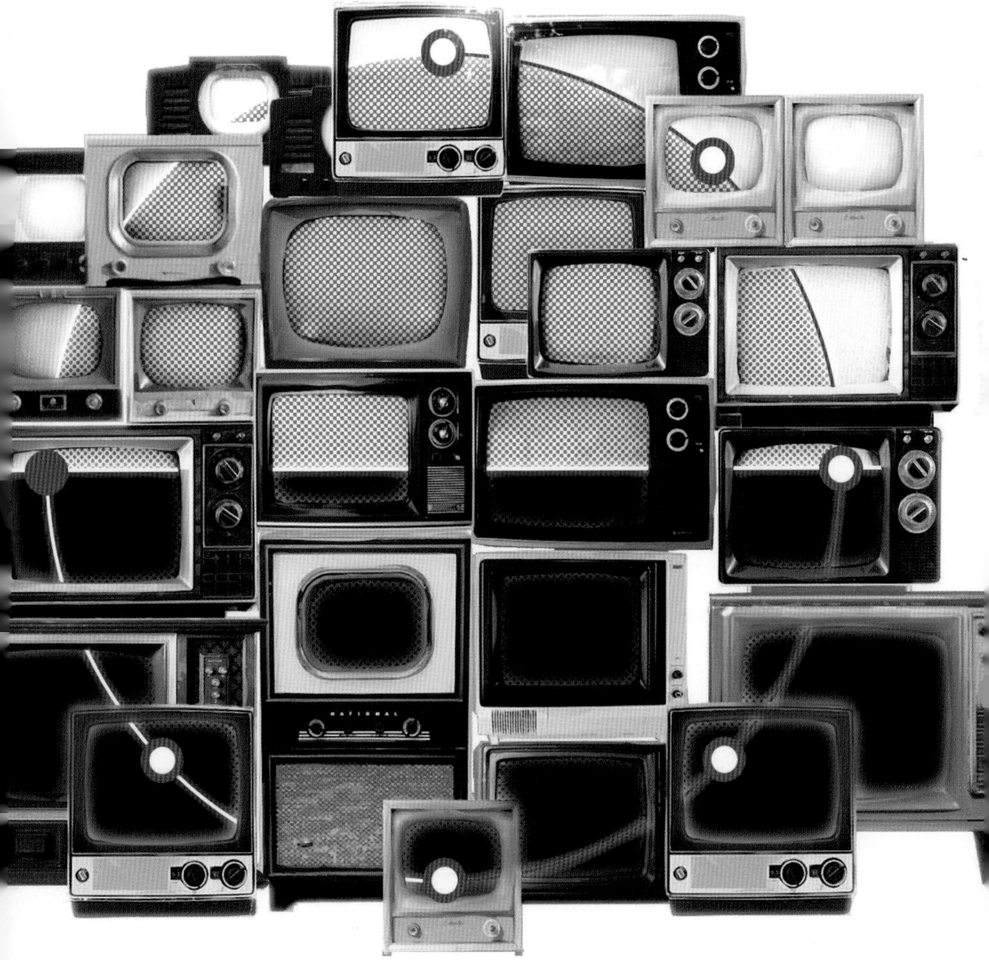

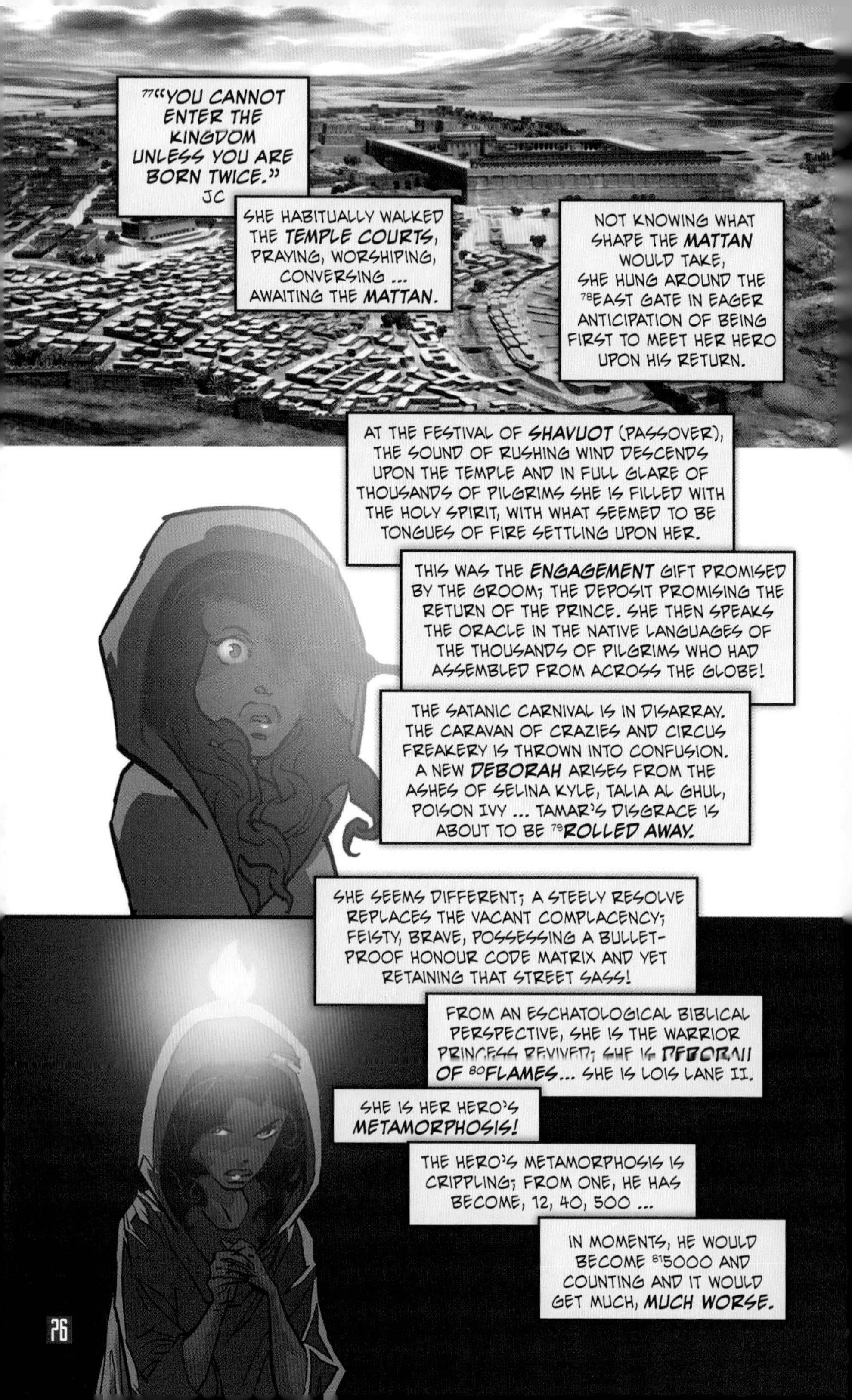
[77]"YOU CANNOT ENTER THE KINGDOM UNLESS YOU ARE BORN TWICE." JC
SHE HABITUALLY WALKED THE ***TEMPLE COURTS***, PRAYING, WORSHIPING, CONVERSING ... AWAITING THE ***MATTAN***.
NOT KNOWING WHAT SHAPE THE ***MATTAN*** WOULD TAKE, SHE HUNG AROUND THE [78]EAST GATE IN EAGER ANTICIPATION OF BEING FIRST TO MEET HER HERO UPON HIS RETURN.
AT THE FESTIVAL OF ***SHAVUOT*** (PASSOVER), THE SOUND OF RUSHING WIND DESCENDS UPON THE TEMPLE AND IN FULL GLARE OF THOUSANDS OF PILGRIMS SHE IS FILLED WITH THE HOLY SPIRIT, WITH WHAT SEEMED TO BE TONGUES OF FIRE SETTLING UPON HER.
THIS WAS THE ***ENGAGEMENT*** GIFT PROMISED BY THE GROOM; THE DEPOSIT PROMISING THE RETURN OF THE PRINCE. SHE THEN SPEAKS THE ORACLE IN THE NATIVE LANGUAGES OF THE THOUSANDS OF PILGRIMS WHO HAD ASSEMBLED FROM ACROSS THE GLOBE!
THE SATANIC CARNIVAL IS IN DISARRAY. THE CARAVAN OF CRAZIES AND CIRCUS FREAKERY IS THROWN INTO CONFUSION. A NEW ***DEBORAH*** ARISES FROM THE ASHES OF SELINA KYLE, TALIA AL GHUL, POISON IVY ... TAMAR'S DISGRACE IS ABOUT TO BE [79]***ROLLED AWAY.***
SHE SEEMS DIFFERENT; A STEELY RESOLVE REPLACES THE VACANT COMPLACENCY; FEISTY, BRAVE, POSSESSING A BULLET-PROOF HONOUR CODE MATRIX AND YET RETAINING THAT STREET SASS!
FROM AN ESCHATOLOGICAL BIBLICAL PERSPECTIVE, SHE IS THE WARRIOR PRINCESS REVIVED; SHE IS ***DEBORAH OF*** [80]***FLAMES***... SHE IS LOIS LANE II.
SHE IS HER HERO'S ***METAMORPHOSIS!***
THE HERO'S METAMORPHOSIS IS CRIPPLING; FROM ONE, HE HAS BECOME, 12, 40, 500 ...
IN MOMENTS, HE WOULD BECOME [81]5000 AND COUNTING AND IT WOULD GET MUCH, ***MUCH WORSE.***

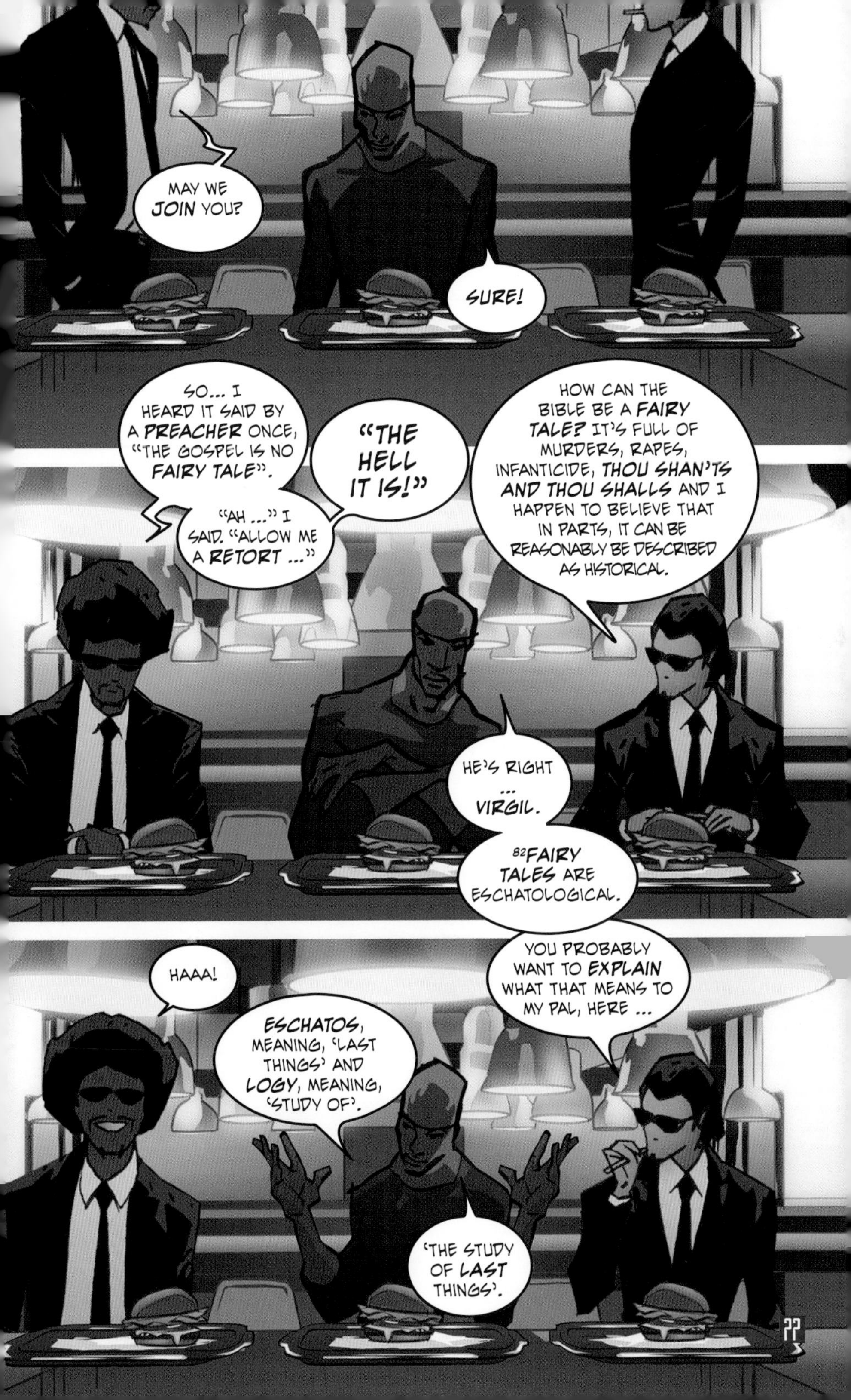
MAY WE JOIN YOU?
SURE!
SO… I HEARD IT SAID BY A PREACHER ONCE, "THE GOSPEL IS NO FAIRY TALE".
"AH …" I SAID. "ALLOW ME A RETORT …"
"THE HELL IT IS!"
HOW CAN THE BIBLE BE A FAIRY TALE? IT'S FULL OF MURDERS, RAPES, INFANTICIDE, THOU SHAN'TS AND THOU SHALLS AND I HAPPEN TO BELIEVE THAT IN PARTS, IT CAN BE REASONABLY BE DESCRIBED AS HISTORICAL.
HE'S RIGHT … VIRGIL.
82FAIRY TALES ARE ESCHATOLOGICAL.
HAAA!
YOU PROBABLY WANT TO EXPLAIN WHAT THAT MEANS TO MY PAL, HERE …
ESCHATOS, MEANING, 'LAST THINGS' AND LOGY, MEANING, 'STUDY OF'.
'THE STUDY OF LAST THINGS'.

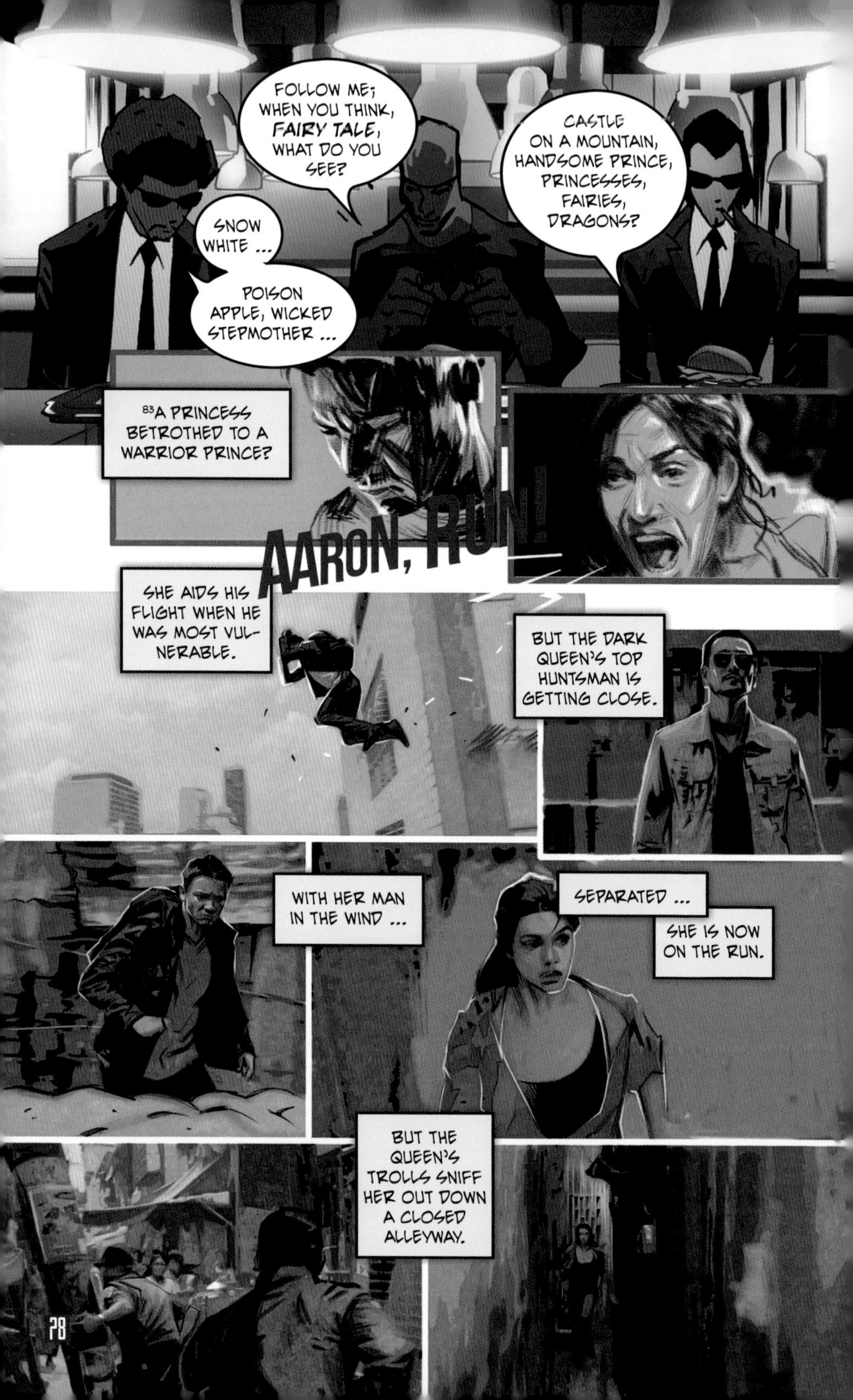
FOLLOW ME; WHEN YOU THINK, FAIRY TALE, WHAT DO YOU SEE?
SNOW WHITE ...
POISON APPLE, WICKED STEPMOTHER ...
CASTLE ON A MOUNTAIN, HANDSOME PRINCE, PRINCESSES, FAIRIES, DRAGONS?
83A PRINCESS BETROTHED TO A WARRIOR PRINCE?
AARON, RUN!
SHE AIDS HIS FLIGHT WHEN HE WAS MOST VUL-NERABLE.
BUT THE DARK QUEEN'S TOP HUNTSMAN IS GETTING CLOSE.
WITH HER MAN IN THE WIND ...
SEPARATED ...
SHE IS NOW ON THE RUN.
BUT THE QUEEN'S TROLLS SNIFF HER OUT DOWN A CLOSED ALLEYWAY.

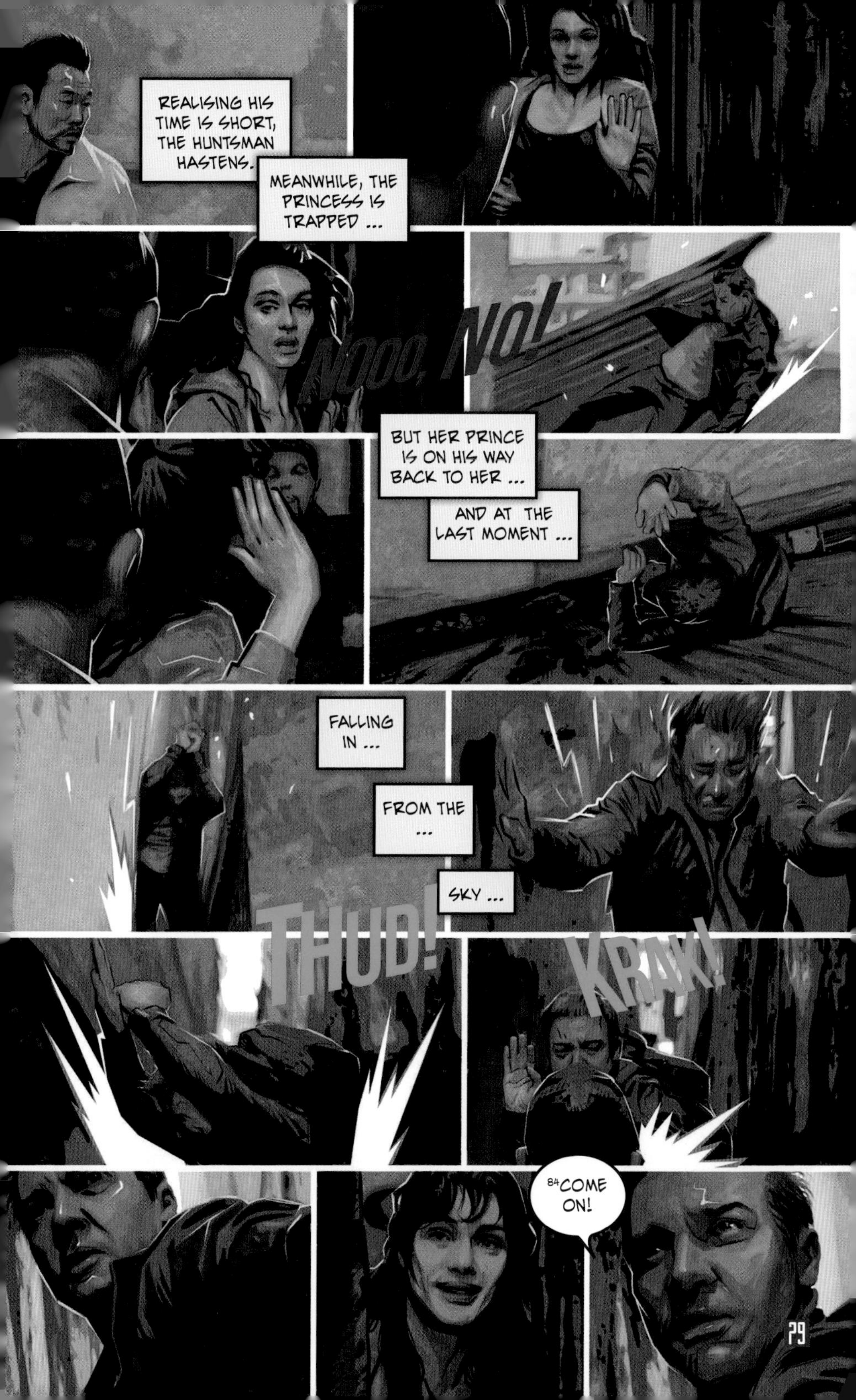
REALISING HIS TIME IS SHORT, THE HUNTSMAN HASTENS.
MEANWHILE, THE PRINCESS IS TRAPPED ...
NOOO, NO!
BUT HER PRINCE IS ON HIS WAY BACK TO HER ...
AND AT THE LAST MOMENT ...
FALLING IN ...
FROM THE ...
SKY ...
THUD!
KRAK!
[84]COME ON!

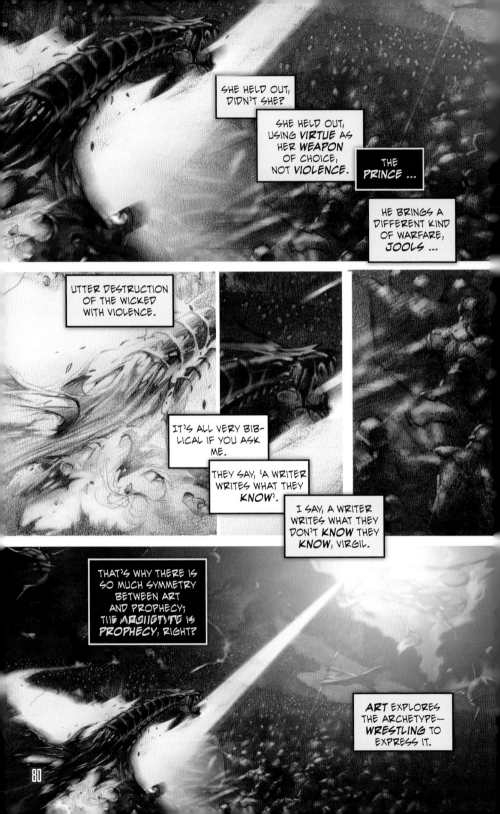

SHE HELD OUT, DIDN'T SHE?

SHE HELD OUT, USING *VIRTUE* AS HER *WEAPON* OF CHOICE, NOT *VIOLENCE.*

THE PRINCE ...

HE BRINGS A DIFFERENT KIND OF WARFARE, *JOOLS* ...

UTTER DESTRUCTION OF THE WICKED WITH VIOLENCE.

IT'S ALL VERY BIB-LICAL IF YOU ASK ME.

THEY SAY, 'A WRITER WRITES WHAT THEY *KNOW'.*

I SAY, A WRITER WRITES WHAT THEY DON'T *KNOW* THEY *KNOW,* VIRGIL.

THAT'S WHY THERE IS SO MUCH SYMMETRY BETWEEN ART AND PROPHECY; THE ARCHTYPE IS PROPHECY, RIGHT?

ART EXPLORES THE ARCHETYPE—*WRESTLING* TO EXPRESS IT.

80

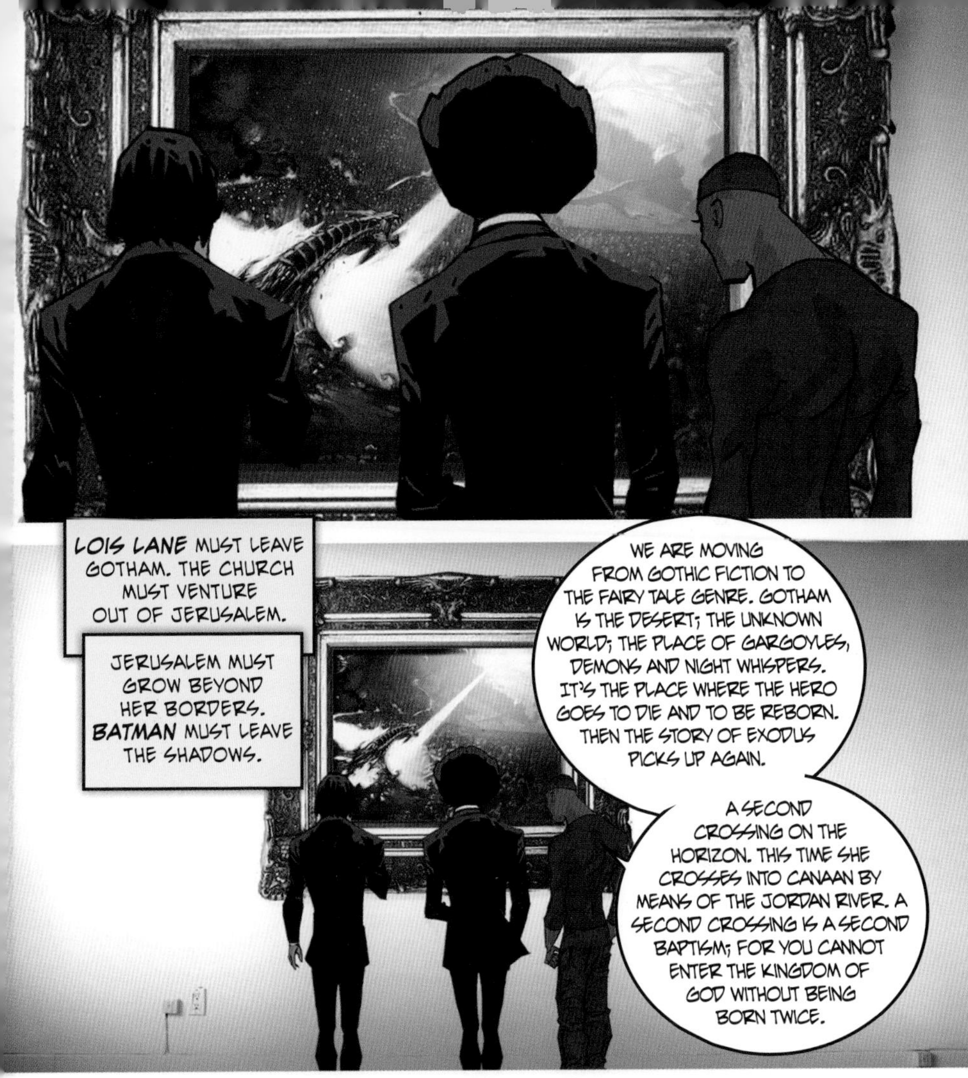
LOIS LANE MUST LEAVE GOTHAM. THE CHURCH MUST VENTURE OUT OF JERUSALEM.
JERUSALEM MUST GROW BEYOND HER BORDERS. BATMAN MUST LEAVE THE SHADOWS.
WE ARE MOVING FROM GOTHIC FICTION TO THE FAIRY TALE GENRE. GOTHAM IS THE DESERT; THE UNKNOWN WORLD; THE PLACE OF GARGOYLES, DEMONS AND NIGHT WHISPERS. IT'S THE PLACE WHERE THE HERO GOES TO DIE AND TO BE REBORN. THEN THE STORY OF EXODUS PICKS UP AGAIN.
A SECOND CROSSING ON THE HORIZON. THIS TIME SHE CROSSES INTO CANAAN BY MEANS OF THE JORDAN RIVER. A SECOND CROSSING IS A SECOND BAPTISM; FOR YOU CANNOT ENTER THE KINGDOM OF GOD WITHOUT BEING BORN TWICE.

TO BE **BORN TWICE** IS TO BE RAISED FROM THE GRAVE ... THAT'S WHAT CROSSING BACK INTO METROPOLIS MEANS.

FROM **EDEN** TO WASTELAND BACK TO **EDEN II**; FROM **LOIS LANE** TO **SELINA KYLE**, BACK TO **LOIS LANE II** ... FOR LOIS LANE AND SELINA KYLE ARE THE **SAME WOMAN.**

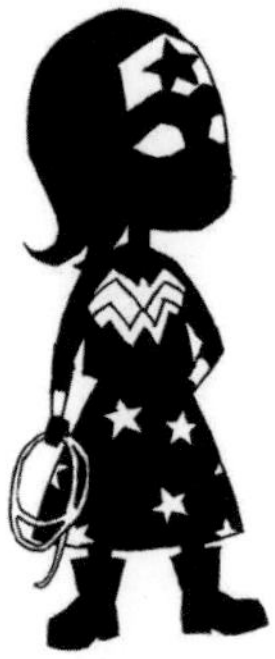

[85]THE **RED DRAGON** HAS BEEN CAST OUT OF HEAVEN; THIS IS A STRATEGIC, FATAL FAILURE. IN HIS SEETHING RAGE, SEEING HIS GAINS RAPIDLY REDUCING TO RUBBLE, HE RUSHES BACK TO THE REALM OF HUMANITY TO WREAK TOTAL WAR ON **JERUSALEM** AND **HER CHILDREN.**

BUT THIS IS NOT THE SAME **LOIS LANE** OF **METROPOLIS**; THIS IS NOT THE SAME **TAMAR** OF **JERUSALEM** FOR THIS ONE IS A SURVIVOR ARMED WITH THE **MATTAN**! (AND THERE ARE SEVERAL HUNDRED **CHILDREN** WITH THE WARRIOR PRINCESS ACROSS THE DIVIDE).

REFERENCES

77. John 3:16.

78. Zechariah 14:4. Ezekiel 43:1-4. Act 5:12.

79. Judges 5:9. The place called 'Gilgal' which is at the Jordan River: meaning the 'rolling away' of disgrace.

80. Deborah of Lapidoth; *Legends of the Jews* 4:2:39. *The Legends of the Jews* by Louis Ginzberg [1909].

81. Take note of the theological significance of the numbers: 12, 40, 50, 120, 5000.

82. Revelation 12, 19:7, 21:2-9.

83. Images and story based on *The Bourne Legacy* (2012). Jeremy Renner as Aaron Cross, Rachel Weisz as Dr Marta Shearing, Loius Ozawa Changchien as LARX #3.

84. The two most persistent motifs in the Bible; first, the messiah's divinity, incarnation and return and the battle for his bride, Jerusalem.

85. Revelation 12.

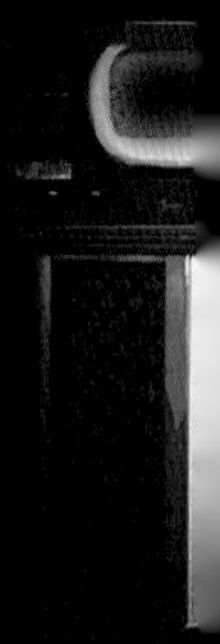

GATE SEVEN

THE WALLS FALL DOWN

RETURN

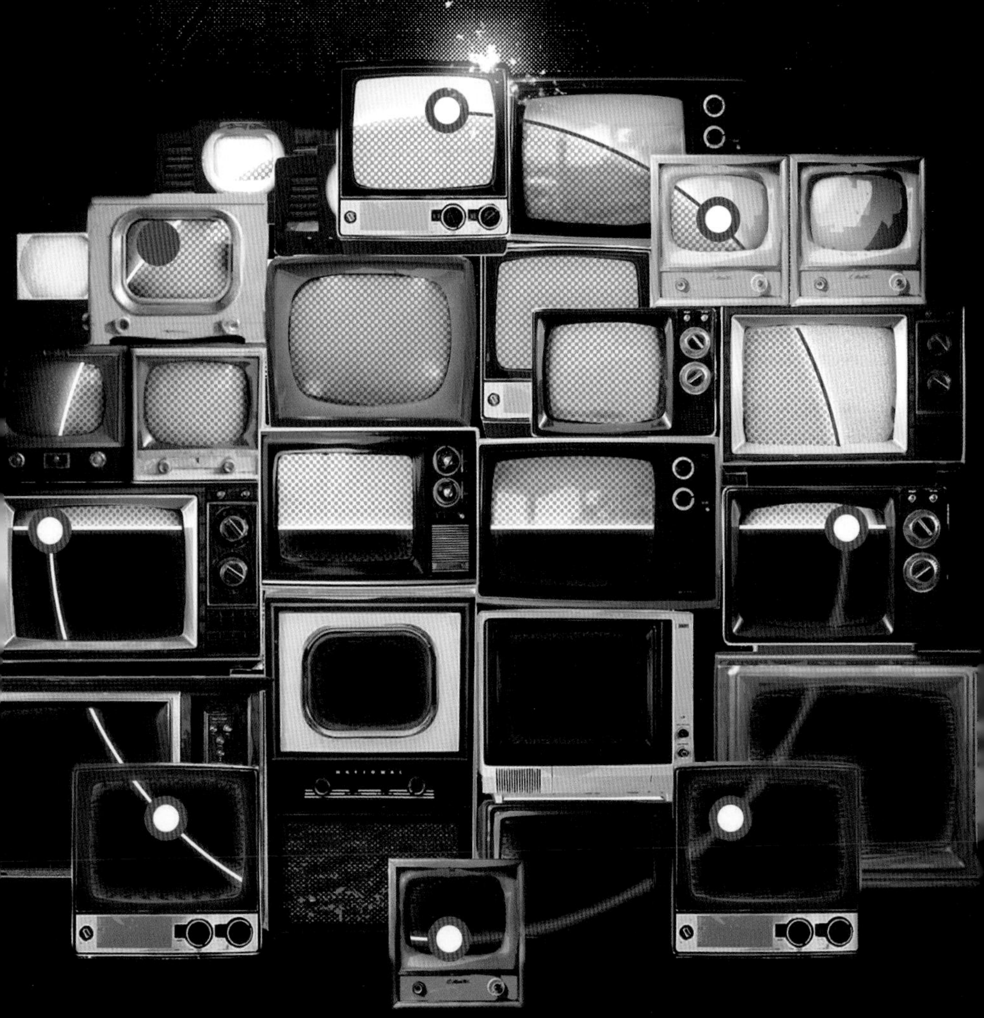

[86]The gap year

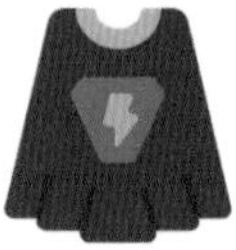

A series of love letters are exchanged between two nobles; a young betrothed and her love. They appear to be exchanging messages during a gap year; that is the period between *erusin* (legal wedding) and *nissuin* (ceremonial wedding).

She writes about their love; laments about snatched moments between palace walls and windows. She initiates correspondence in response to his work in the lower regions where he raised her from slavery and death.

To her detractors; the unbelievers ... the nations, she explains:

[87]Do not stare at me because I am swarthy,
it is the sun that has burnt me.
[88]My mother's sons were angry with me,
they made me tend the vineyards.
My own vineyard I did not tend!

She makes reference to her kin and kind; the sages would suggest these characters to be Egyptians persecuting Israel in the days of Ramses. From a christologically messianic perspective however, these sound like Joseph's brothers and the Jewish authorities who persecuted the Jerusalem church.

She is clearly emerging from that phase of persecution and spite when her lover, the newly-crowned prince announces himself and calls her away from the rebellious rabble.

[89]I am a rose of Sharon,
a lily of the valleys.
lily among thistles,
so is my love among [90]girls.
[91]Come then, my love,
my lovely one, come.
For see, winter is past,
the rains are over and gone.
[92]Catch the foxes for us,
the little foxes that ruin the vineyards,
for our vineyards are in fruit.

There are other voices (chorus) in the discourse; shepherds, the nations and [93]the council of God; the nations gasp at the sight of the warrior princess ascending out of the desert, at the edge of the divide:

[94]Who is she that comes up from the desert
Like columns of smoke,
In clouds of myrrh and frankincense,
Of all the powders of the merchant?
[95]Who is this coming in from the desert
leaning on her beloved?

Having transformed from victim to virgin warrior, traversing the desolate place, reaching the borders of the land of promise. She recalls her husband's valour and love in the desert places:

[96]*His left hand was under my head,*
His right arm embraced me.
[97]*I compare you, my love,*
to a mare among Pharaoh's chariots.

The young king responds as he recalls the moment of *mohar* as they became engaged.

[98]*You ravish my heart,*
my sister, my bride,
you ravish my heart
with one glance of your eyes,
with one jewel of your necklace.

In melodramatic fashion, he continues,

I sleep but my heart is awake.
The sound of my lover knocking!
[99]*Open to me, my sister, my love,*
my dove, my perfect one,
for my head is wet with dew,
[100]*my hair with the drops of the night.*

She rushes to the door in response,

101I opened to my love,
but my love had turned and gone.

102She rushes to seize him, but he must leave so he can send her the *mattan*. She receives the *mattan* and begins to flourish; she bore and adopted children of promise, swelling her ranks to the dismay of the power brokers.

103The watchmen met me, those who go around the city. They beat me, they wounded me, they took my cloak away from me, those guardians of the ramparts! 104I charge you, 105daughters of Jerusalem, if you should find my love, what should you tell him? That I am sick with love!

To which the nations (maidens of Jerusalem) respond,

What makes your love the best?
Why is your lover better than other lovers,
O loveliest of women?
Why is your lover better than other lovers,
to put us under such an oath?

She replies,

His belly a block of ivory
covered with sapphires.
Such is my love, such is my friend,
O daughters of Jerusalem.

The nations continue,
[106]O loveliest of women?
Which way did your lover turn
so that we can help you seek him?

Is this an honest request from the nations? Has my love for my king won them over? She replies using motifs from the first gardener, Adam. Her man, Adam II is playing the archetype: he is away at work, just like his father … never stops working; establishing his rule, subduing worlds;

[107]My love went down to his garden,
to the beds of spices,
to pasture his flock on the grass
and gather lilies.

In the final lines of correspondence, she calls unto her lover,

[100]Haste away, my love, be like a gazelle,
a young stag, on the [110]on the mountains of spice.

"Hurry, my love; I will join you at the Temple Mount in the new kingdom!"

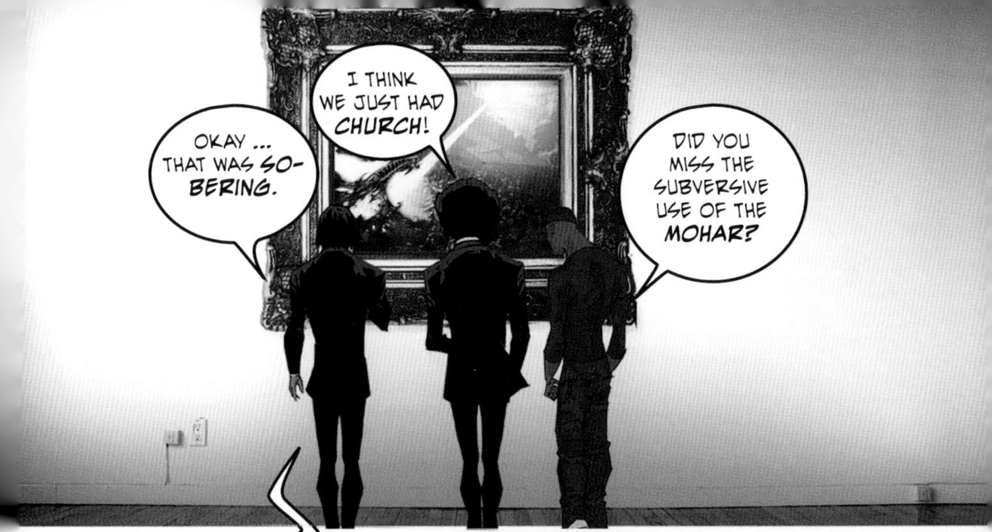
OKAY ... THAT WAS SOBERING.
I THINK WE JUST HAD CHURCH!
DID YOU MISS THE SUBVERSIVE USE OF THE MOHAR?

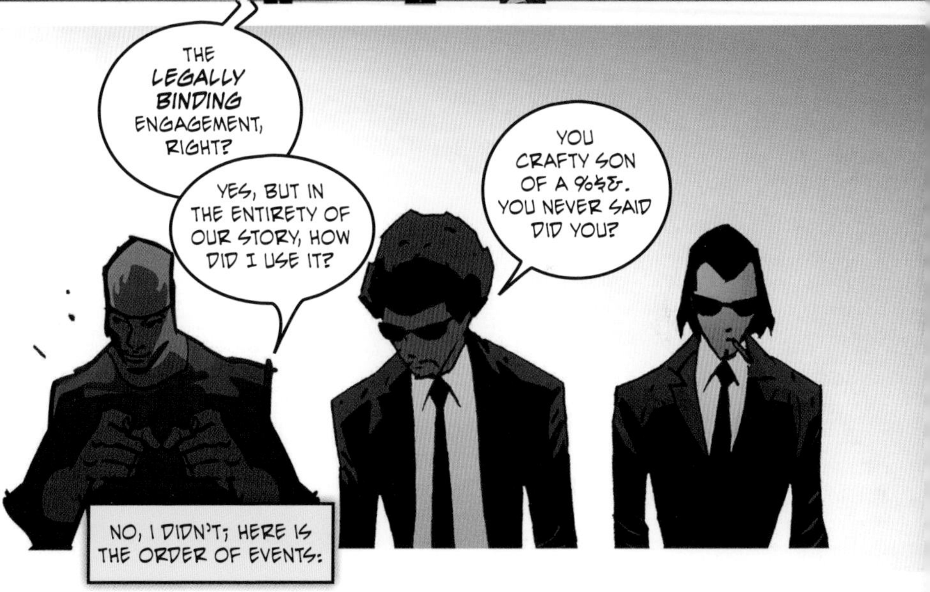
THE LEGALLY BINDING ENGAGEMENT, RIGHT?
YES, BUT IN THE ENTIRETY OF OUR STORY, HOW DID I USE IT?
YOU CRAFTY SON OF A %$&. YOU NEVER SAID DID YOU?
NO, I DIDN'T; HERE IS THE ORDER OF EVENTS:

Kiddushin – *matchmaking*; God presents himself to Israel at Sinai.

Ketubah – *marriage contract;* God ratifies the law in the desert with the people's consent. It is renewed at the Lord's Supper.

Erusin – *legal marriage;* Jesus arrives to consumate marriage but is betrayed and murdered.

Mohar – *dowry* payment from father.

Mattan – *gift from groom to bride;* the gift of the Holy Spirit.

Nissuin – *ceremonial marriage* at the end of time.

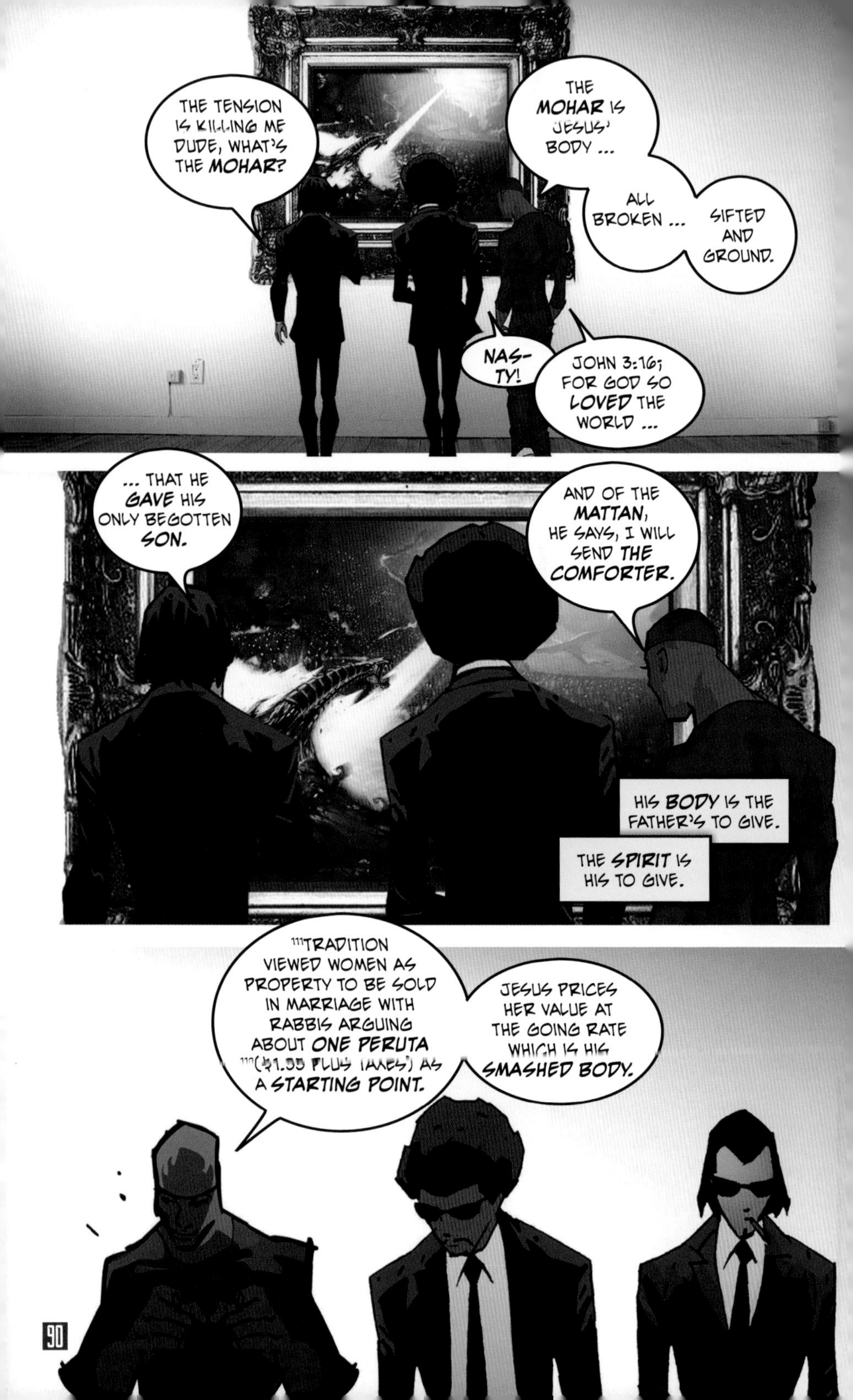
THE TENSION IS KILLING ME DUDE, WHAT'S THE **MOHAR**?
THE **MOHAR** IS JESUS' BODY ...
ALL BROKEN ...
SIFTED AND GROUND.
NAS-TY!
JOHN 3:16; FOR GOD SO ***LOVED*** THE WORLD ...
... THAT HE ***GAVE*** HIS ONLY BEGOTTEN ***SON***.
AND OF THE **MATTAN**, HE SAYS, I WILL SEND **THE COMFORTER**.
HIS ***BODY*** IS THE FATHER'S TO GIVE.
THE ***SPIRIT*** IS HIS TO GIVE.
[111]TRADITION VIEWED WOMEN AS PROPERTY TO BE SOLD IN MARRIAGE WITH RABBIS ARGUING ABOUT ***ONE PERUTA*** [112]($1.55 PLUS TAXES) AS A ***STARTING POINT***.
JESUS PRICES HER VALUE AT THE GOING RATE WHICH IS HIS ***SMASHED BODY***.

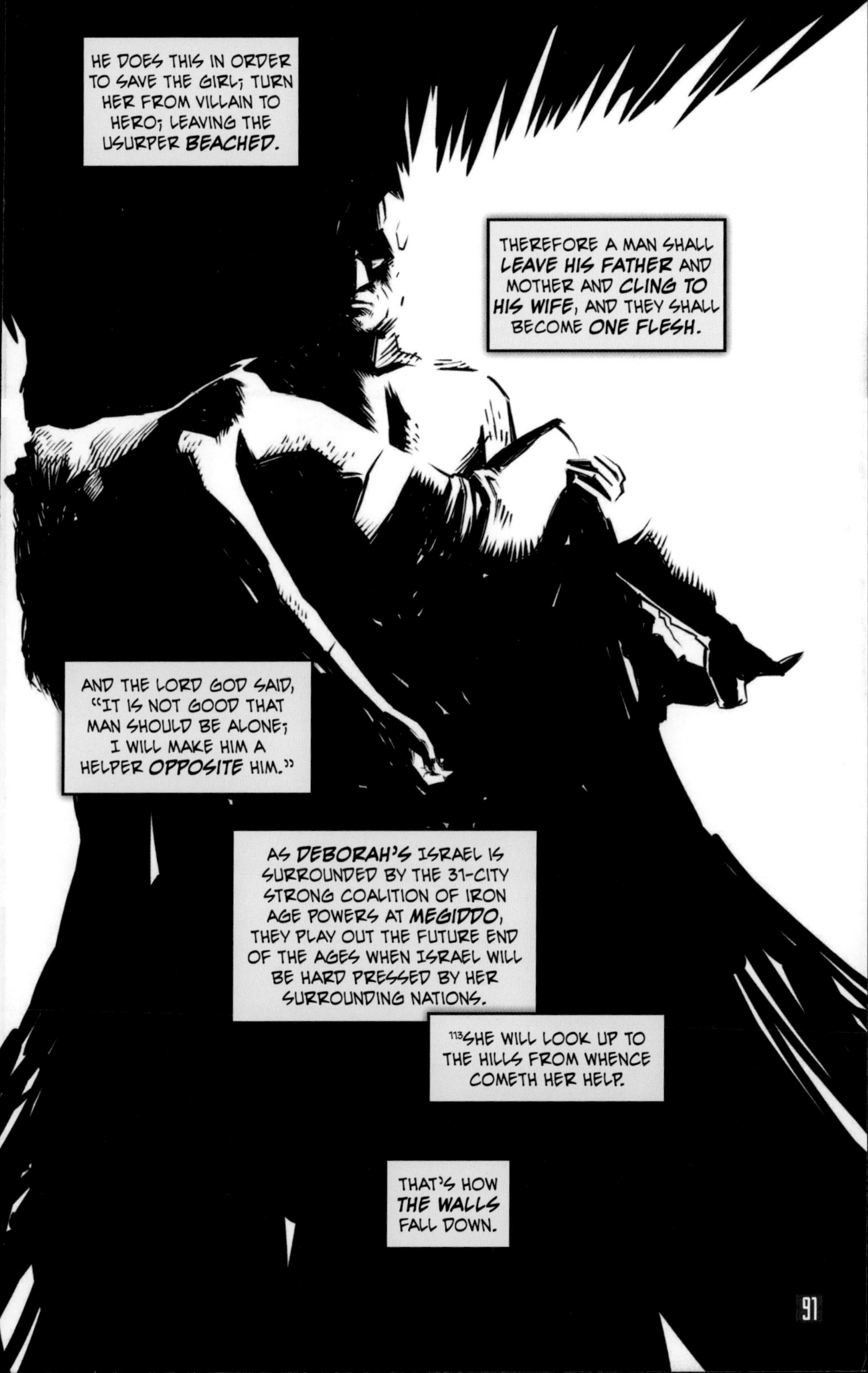
HE DOES THIS IN ORDER TO SAVE THE GIRL; TURN HER FROM VILLAIN TO HERO; LEAVING THE USURPER BEACHED.
THEREFORE A MAN SHALL LEAVE HIS FATHER AND MOTHER AND CLING TO HIS WIFE, AND THEY SHALL BECOME ONE FLESH.
AND THE LORD GOD SAID, "IT IS NOT GOOD THAT MAN SHOULD BE ALONE; I WILL MAKE HIM A HELPER OPPOSITE HIM."
AS DEBORAH'S ISRAEL IS SURROUNDED BY THE 31-CITY STRONG COALITION OF IRON AGE POWERS AT MEGIDDO, THEY PLAY OUT THE FUTURE END OF THE AGES WHEN ISRAEL WILL BE HARD PRESSED BY HER SURROUNDING NATIONS.
[113]SHE WILL LOOK UP TO THE HILLS FROM WHENCE COMETH HER HELP.
THAT'S HOW THE WALLS FALL DOWN.

REFERENCES

86. A New Testament read of *Song of Songs*. Translation (unless indicated), *The Revised New Jerusalem Bible.* Darton Longman and Todd. 2019. The Hebrew sages viewed *Songs of Solomon* as the *Song of Songs* sang when Israel left Egypt. See Exodus 15.

87. Songs 1:6.

88. She is the only girl in the family; read what you may into that. Her own kin would persecute her; see persecutors of kin archetypes: Joseph's brothers, Cain, Esau?

89. Songs 2:1, 2.

90. The maidens; metaphor for 'the nations'. See Rashi (Daughters of Jerusalem). See also New Testament references: Luke 8:7, Hebrews 6:8, Matthew 13:30, 38.

91. Songs 2: 10, 11. Come with me across the Jordan!

92. Songs 2: 15; Compare with Judges 15 for the Jesus/Samson archetype.

93. Songs 1:11.

94. Songs 3:6. Translation, *Tanakh: The Holy Scriptures,* published by JPS. Source: jps.org. License: Copyright: JPS, 1985.

95. Songs 8:5.

96. Songs 2:6. Translation, *Tanakh: The Holy Scriptures.* Rashi: He traveled a three-days' journey to search out a resting place for them. See Bamidbar 10:33, "And in that resting place, He brought down manna and quails for them. All this I remember now in my exile, and I am sick for His love."

97. Songs 1:9 (Evidence that the Exodus story is the narrative backdrop to this romantic framework). A Samson/Israel vs Philistine Power paradigm is also a useful template.

98. Songs 4:9, 5:2.

99. Revelation 3:20.

100. Songs 5:2. Rashi commentary: "For my head is drenched [as though] with dew," because I am full of good will and satisfaction with Avrohom your forefather, whose deeds were pleasing to Me as dew. And behold, I come to you, laden with blessings and the payment of reward for good deeds if you return to Me.

101. Songs 5:6.

102. John 16:7.

103. Religious authorities, gentile nations, landed interests who struck down Jesus and struck down the church. Rabbinical commentary suggests the watchmen here are Nebuchanezzer, the irony is clear.

104. Songs 5:8-9.

105. Rashi comments: [Scripture] calls the nations, "the daughters תוֹנְב of Yerusholayim" because it is destined to become the metropolis for them all, as Yechezkeil prophesied, "I will give them to you as surrounding villages תוֹנָבְל," Yechezkeil 16:61. And similarly, "Ekron, and its suburbs הָיֶתוֹנְבוּ." Yehoshua 15:45. The Metsudah Five Megillot, Lakewood, N.J., 2001.

106. Songs 6: 1-2.

107. Genesis 2:15, cp. 1:28.

108. Songs 8:14.

109. Hurry, take me home!

110. Anticipating the rebuilding of the Temple Mount; spices refer to the Temple incense fragrances.

111. Kiddusin 12a (The Talmud). A lengthy debate on the value of a bride is engaged. Jesus short-circuits this idiosyncratic vestige of the ancient world.

112. A Peruta is 0.025 of a gram of silver [$0.57 per gram-November 2021]. https://shulchanaruchharav.com/wp-content/uploads/2017/01/Peruta-value-website.pdf

113. Psalm 121:1.

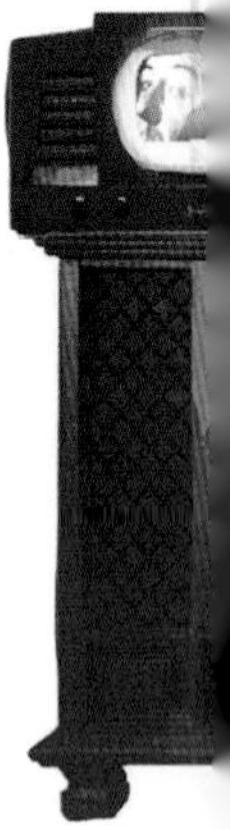

GATE ZERO

ORIGINS DESTINY

A NEW ADVENTURE BEGINS...

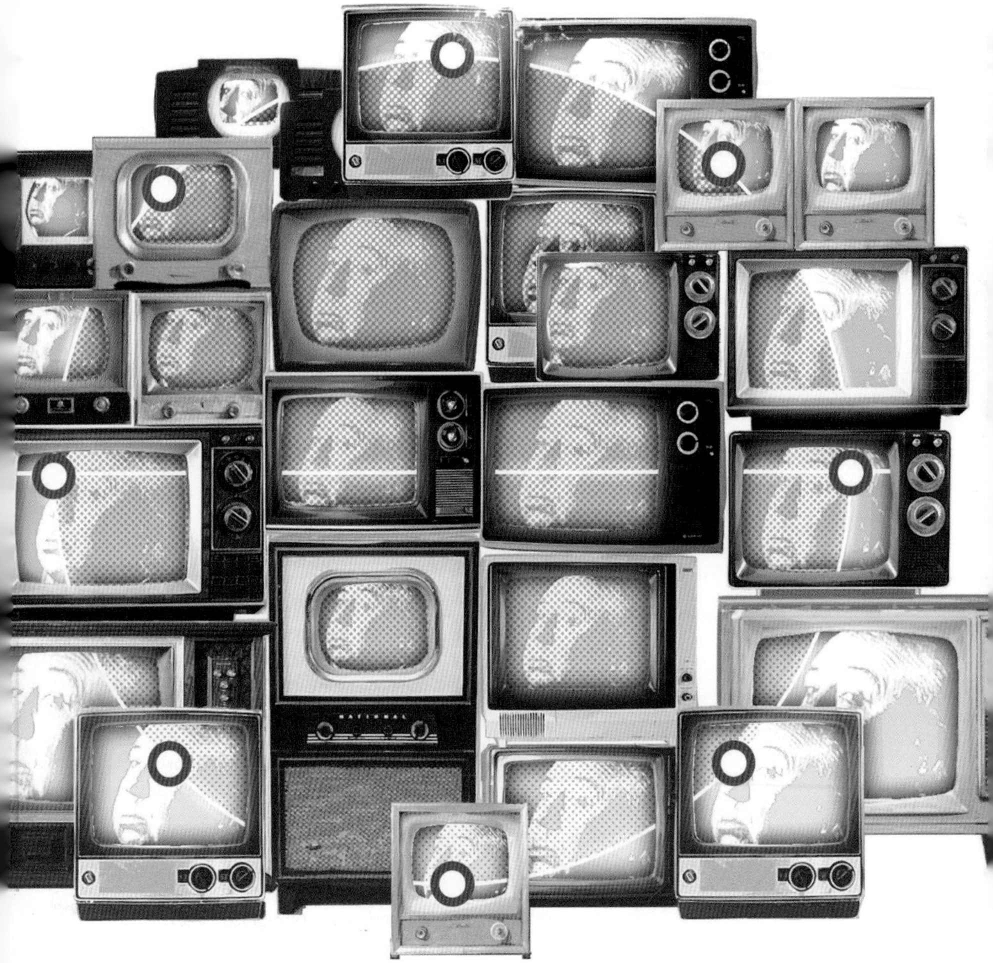
NATIONAL

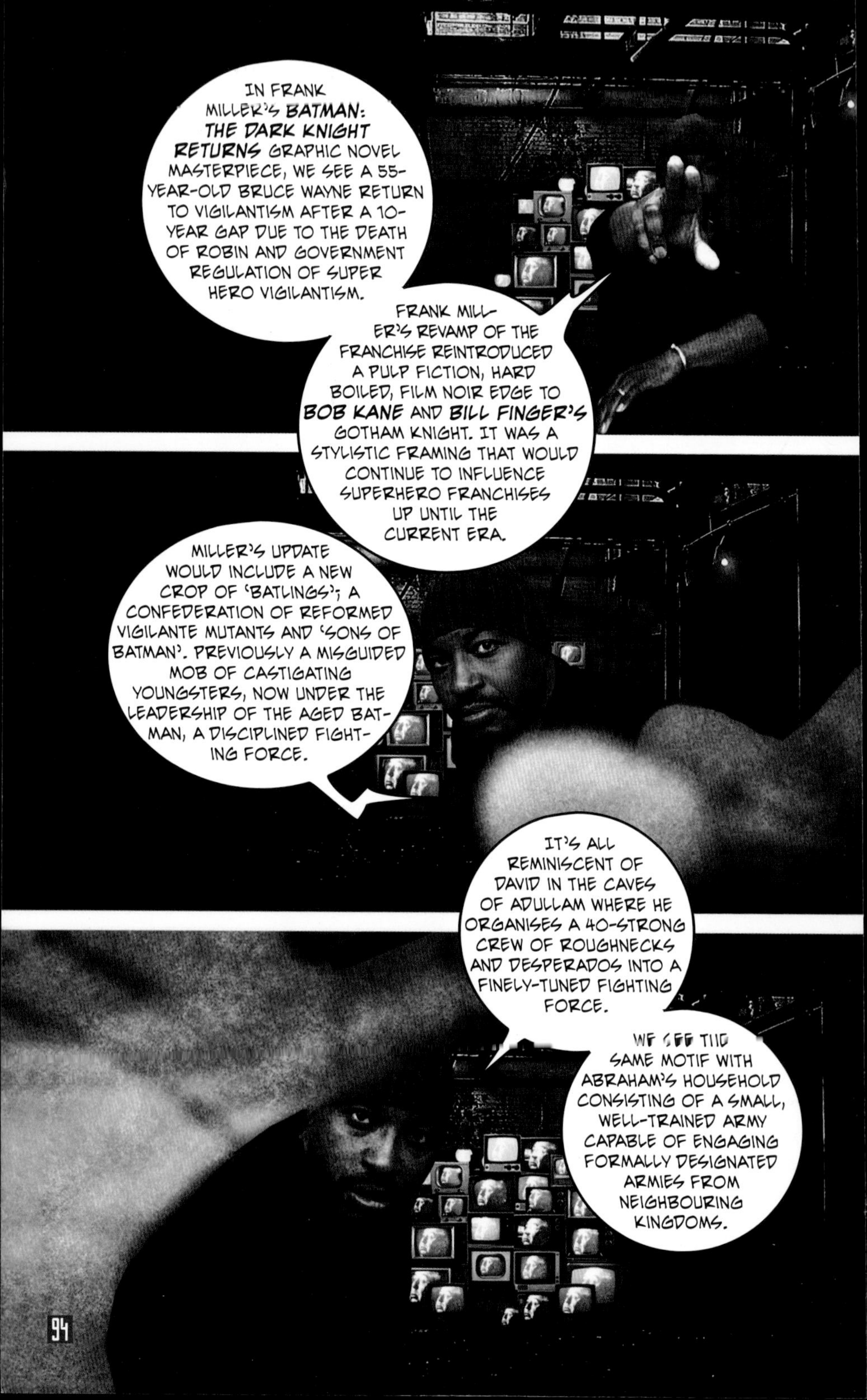
IN FRANK MILLER'S **BATMAN: THE DARK KNIGHT RETURNS** GRAPHIC NOVEL MASTERPIECE, WE SEE A 55-YEAR-OLD BRUCE WAYNE RETURN TO VIGILANTISM AFTER A 10-YEAR GAP DUE TO THE DEATH OF ROBIN AND GOVERNMENT REGULATION OF SUPER HERO VIGILANTISM.
FRANK MILLER'S REVAMP OF THE FRANCHISE REINTRODUCED A PULP FICTION, HARD BOILED, FILM NOIR EDGE TO **BOB KANE** AND **BILL FINGER'S** GOTHAM KNIGHT. IT WAS A STYLISTIC FRAMING THAT WOULD CONTINUE TO INFLUENCE SUPERHERO FRANCHISES UP UNTIL THE CURRENT ERA.
MILLER'S UPDATE WOULD INCLUDE A NEW CROP OF 'BATLINGS'; A CONFEDERATION OF REFORMED VIGILANTE MUTANTS AND 'SONS OF BATMAN'. PREVIOUSLY A MISGUIDED MOB OF CASTIGATING YOUNGSTERS, NOW UNDER THE LEADERSHIP OF THE AGED BATMAN, A DISCIPLINED FIGHTING FORCE.
IT'S ALL REMINISCENT OF DAVID IN THE CAVES OF ADULLAM WHERE HE ORGANISES A 40-STRONG CREW OF ROUGHNECKS AND DESPERADOS INTO A FINELY-TUNED FIGHTING FORCE.
WE SEE THE SAME MOTIF WITH ABRAHAM'S HOUSEHOLD CONSISTING OF A SMALL, WELL-TRAINED ARMY CAPABLE OF ENGAGING FORMALLY DESIGNATED ARMIES FROM NEIGHBOURING KINGDOMS.

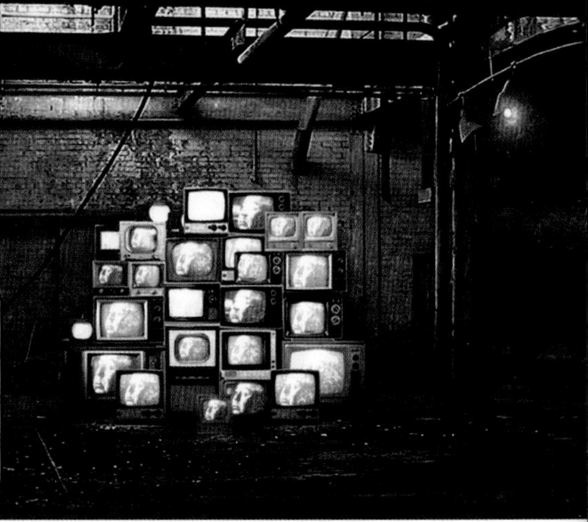

WE PUSH THIS ARCHETYPE A TAD FURTHER. AS OUR WARRIOR PRINCESS CROSSES THE BORDER INTO CIVILISATION, SHE IS ACCOMPANIED BY A HOST OF CHILDREN.

LIKE THE SCENES FROM DISNEY'S ***THE MANDALORIAN*** OR ***MAD MAX: BEYOND THUNDERDOME'S*** [114]'LOST TRIBE', SHE PROBABLY HAS THE YOUNGEST CHILD STRAPPED TO HER BACK, SWORD IN HAND.

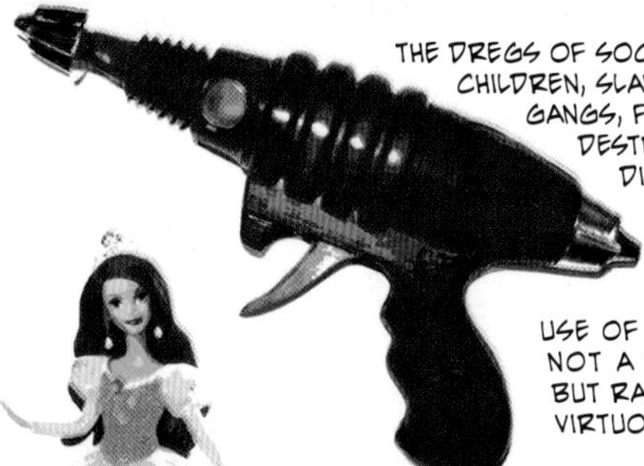

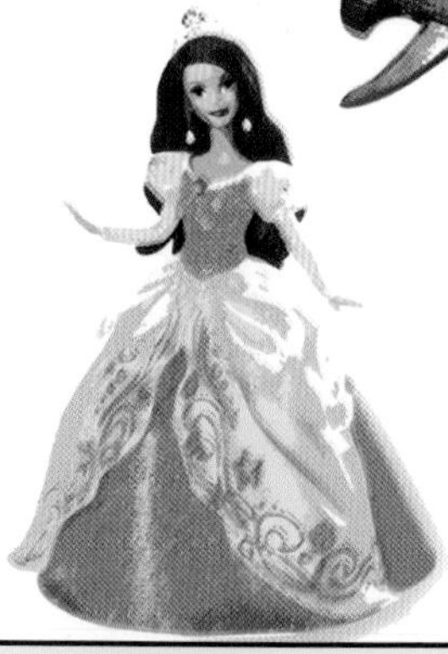

THE DREGS OF SOCIETY, STREET CHILDREN, LOST CHILDREN, SLAVES OF EVERY SORT; STREET GANGS, FORGOTTEN SORTS, ABUSED AND DESTROYED. SHE FORMS THEM INTO A DISCIPLINED, VIRTUOUS FIGHTING FORCE; THEY ARE NOW HER OWN CHILDREN. ADOPTED INTO HER BODY AS A CHILD IS PART OF HER MOTHER'S BODY. FOR ALL THE USE OF MARTIAL METAPHOR, HERS IS NOT A BATTLE OF ARMED ENGAGEMENT, BUT RATHER ONE OF FORTHTELLING AND VIRTUOUS LIVING.

SHE COMES FULL CIRCLE BACK TO WHERE IT ALL BEGAN; PROMISED TO AND BELOVED OF THE CROWN PRINCE. THE BATTLE-WORN ARMOUR EXCHANGED FOR A BRIDAL TRAIN; HER BRUISES FROM BATTLE WILL BE WASHED IN LIVING WATERS AND PERFUMED IN SCENTED OILS FROM THE TREE OF LIFE AS SHE IS PRESENTED TO HER ETERNALLY BETROTHED HUSBAND.

NEITHER BRIDE OR GROOM ARE THE SAME AS AT THIS POINT AT THE BEGINNING OF THE JOURNEY; HE IS ***GOD-MAN*** ENTHRONED AND SHE IS SOMETHING NEW IN THE UNIVERSES; ONE, RESURRECTED FROM THE DEAD INTO A GLORIOUS BODY.

HIS CORONATION AND HER WEDDING, FINALLY CEREMONIALLY CONFIRMED.

OF THE KING AND HIS QUEEN, IT IS SAID, ***THEY LIVED HAPPILY EVER AFTER.***

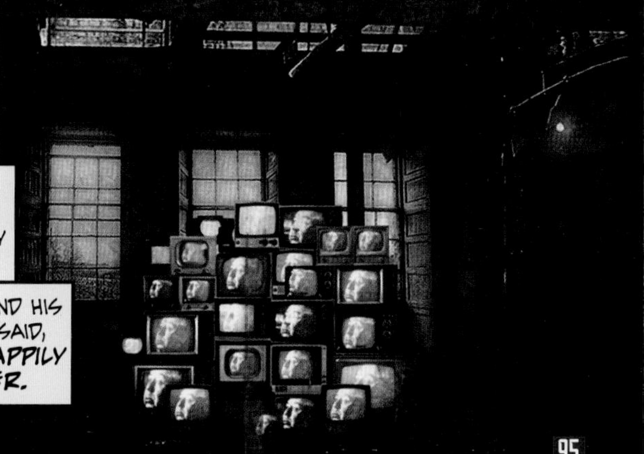

REFERENCES

114. A tribe of children who survived the apocalypse and thrived in a desert oasis in the third instalment of the *Mad Max* movie franchise. Mad Max was apparently destined to lead them to the fabled utopic, Tomorrow-Morrow Land.

NOTES

CAST

MAIN PLAYERS

JESUS, BATMAN, JERUSALEM, ALFRED HITCHCOCK, SUPERMAN, PRINCESS TAMAR, GOMER, LOIS LANE, SELINA KYLE, TALIA AL GHUL, RA'S AL GHUL, JOHN THE BAPTISER, POISON IVY, JOKER, HOSEA, ABSALOM, AMNON, SAMSON, FRANK MILLER, BOB KANE, BILL FINGER, SIKU, JANET & AJIBAYO AKINSIKU SNR.

RABBINICAL COMMENTARY:

RABBI SHLOMO YITZCHAKI (RASHI). RASHI LIVED IN TROYES, FRANCE (1040-1105).

THE BOURNE LEGACY (2012):

JEREMY RENNER AS AARON CROSS

RACHEL WEISZ AS DR MARTA SHEARING

LOUIS OZAWA CHANGCHIEN AS LARX #3

SIKU CONTACT:

GO STUDIO: gostudio.us, info@gostudio.us

PERSONAL: theartofsiku.com, siku@theartofsiku.com

SOCIAL MEDIA HANDLE: theartofsiku

DRINK IT BIBLE COURSE GRAPHIC NOVEL: kingdomvsempire.org

Look out for accompanying music and podcast links at Go Studio website.

GO STUDIO PARTNERS:

Global Catalytic Ministries: catalyticministries.com

Frontier Alliance International: faimission.org

Joel Richardson: joelstrumpet.com

Tunnel Vision: tunnelvisiongoggles.com

FAI Studio: faistudios.org

MEDSiS: Medsis.com

Storm Payments: StormPayments.app

MUM'S GRIOT RECITATION FROM PAGE 9:

YouTube: Siku Mum, the Griot

https://youtu.be/tuKKJmoZf3A

ICON IMAGES: pages 26, 46 & 84: Flaticon.com. Icon design resources from Flaticon.com